Disney

PRINCESS COOKIE PARTY

Disney PRINCESS COOKIE PARTY

50+ FAMILY-FRIENDLY RECIPES INSPIRED BY YOUR FAVORITE DISNEY PRINCESSES

By Sarah Walker Caron

INSIGHT
EDITIONS

SAN RAFAEL • LOS ANGELES • LONDON

CONTENTS

CHAPTER 3

CLASSIC COOKIES

CHAPTER 4

BROWNIES AND BARS

CHAPTER 5

SPECIALTY COOKIES

INTRODUCTION

Nothing quite compares to the magical feeling of seeing Tiana fulfill her dream of opening a restaurant in New Orleans, or the joy experienced when Mulan cleverly defeats the Huns, or the exhilaration of watching the dragons fly through the sky as Raya hugs her family.

For decades now, the Disney Princesses have been inspiring fans to follow their dreams while still remaining true to themselves. The Princesses are so much more than animated characters—each one embodies qualities that resonate across time, cultures, and age.

Just think of all the hope and joy Snow White, Cinderella, Aurora, and Raya have brought to us. Or how Ariel, Belle, and Jasmine always kept their curiosity alive, despite outside forces working against them. We witnessed the courage and bravery of Pocahontas, Mulan, and Tiana, while Merida, Moana, and Rapunzel showed us how to embrace our independence and vibrancy.

What better way to celebrate the friendship and connection that the Disney Princesses bring to the world than with the ultimate Disney Princess Cookie Party! These 50 recipes, all inspired by the Princesses' stories, are guides for creating sweet, delicious, memorable cookies perfect for enjoying with friends and loved ones.

From Carriage Pumpkin Chocolate Chip Cookies inspired by Cinderella's evening at the ball, or swirled Heart of Te Fiti Cookies honoring Moana's journey to save her people, to Blueberry Beignets celebrating Tiana's success, there is a royal recipe for every Princess!

Grab your own favorite Princess-worthy apron, put on your tiara, and roll up your sleeves. It's time to bring a little Princess magic into your kitchen!

Fables
Fairy Tales

TIPS, TRICKS, AND TOOLS FOR PRINCESS-PERFECT COOKIE BAKING

Every princess knows that the right tools are key to successful baking. Whether you are a novice baker or a seasoned pro, these basic tools will guarantee that all your Disney Princess cookies are royal perfection.

NONSTICK BAKING SHEET For even baking that ensures your cookies have beautiful golden edges and perfectly baked centers, a nonstick baking sheet is the way to go. All the recipes in this book were tested using several baking sheet styles, but this type provided the best and most consistent results.

PARCHMENT PAPER Line baking sheets with parchment paper for even baking. All the cookies in this book were baked on nonstick baking sheets lined with parchment paper. Cut the paper to fit whatever size baking sheet you are using.

STAND MIXER OR HANDHELD MIXER Although many recipes in this book call for a stand mixer, all can be made with a handhand mixer as well. Mixers are important for transforming butter, sugar, and other ingredients into sweet treats.

AN 8-BY-8-INCH GLASS BAKING DISH For bar cookies, a glass baking dish will provide the most even bake. Although these recipes were tested in other pans, the 8-by-8-inch glass baking dish consistently produced results worthy of the royal court.

GEL FOOD COLORING Gel food coloring imbues rich, brilliant colors without adding any liquid to the dough, frosting, or icing, ensuring perfect consistency.

COOKIE SCOOPS IN SMALL, MEDIUM, AND LARGE For cookies to be consistent in size and shape, cookie scoops are a must. They make quick work of portioning out dough for all your baking recipes.

FOR BEST RESULTS

READ THE RECIPE BEFORE YOU BEGIN. Reading the recipe all the way through (including the ingredients list!) will help you prepare for all the steps that follow.

ALWAYS PREHEAT THE OVEN THOROUGHLY. Bringing the oven up to the designated temperature before beginning to bake will ensure that cookies are baked under optimal conditions.

ENSURE THAT YOUR INGREDIENTS ARE THE RIGHT TEMPERATURE. In many recipes, butter (and sometimes eggs!) need to be at room temperature to produce the best dough; other recipes require ingredients to be cold. These details are key to preparing the dough and baking the best cookies. Take note of any instructions like this before you begin a recipe.

SET A TIMER. Every princess knows that a timer is a failsafe reminder to take your cookies out of the oven once they've been baked to perfection.

HOW TO HOST A PRINCESS COOKIE PARTY

If you want to celebrate all that's incredible about the Disney Princesses, a cookie party is the perfect way to do so. Here's what you need to plan your perfect party.

INVITATIONS It is a royal honor to be invited to such a gathering. When inviting guests, you'll want to follow the lead of the palace in wording your invitation. May we suggest: "You are cordially invited to the Royal Cookie Ball held in honor of Princess [Name] on [Date]. Wear your finest royal attire and direct your carriage to [Address] for a magical day of cookie decorating."

Or, if you are planning an adventure-themed cookie party, try this wording: "We invite you on a quest through an enchanted realm of cookies and confections to celebrate Princess [Name]. At the Princess Cookie Party, brave guests will battle frosting and sprinkles to create a magical array of cookies. Won't you join us on [Date] at [Location]?"

Perhaps you want to lean more into whimsy with the following wording: "A world of sparkling wishes and imaginative creations awaits. You are invited to a Princess Cookie Party in honor of Princess [Name], where you'll put whimsy and dreams to work making creative cookies galore. Won't you join us on [Date] at [location]?"

SETTING THE SCENE A princess thinks through all the details. Cover the table with your favorite princess colors (pink, blue, lavender, yellow, green—you choose!). Lay out perfect platters and cake stands for cookies. Add twinkling lights (tiny strands in glass jars are always a nice touch!), tiaras, and other finery for the royal guests. Your soundtrack is your favorite Disney Princess songs. And don't forget to have costume accessories on hand, such as princess shoes, jewelry, and capes, so the guests can add to their princess perfection.

Interested in a more adventurous vibe? If your theme is more adventurous, lean into earth tones for your color scheme, and don't forget the maps, binoculars, bows, and suction-cup arrows. For a dreamier take on décor, stick to the blues and whites and make sure there are plenty of ballons and pom-poms.

ROYAL COOKIE DECORATING Before the party, bake sugar cookies in princess-themed shapes—think tiaras, dresses, shoes, and plaques. Prepare royal icing and set out piping bags for your royal guests to use. Have sprinkles, edible glitter, and other decorations on hand. Set the party table with plates and arrange 3 to 4 cookies on each. Guests then choose a cookie and use their favorite icing to outline and fill it. Add sprinkles and decorations while the icing is still wet, then arrange the cookies on the plate to harden. Remember, there is no wrong way to decorate a princess cookie!

ROYAL SNACKING Set the royal snack table with additional treats and punch fit for princesses! Fruit skewers, vegetables and dip, tiny sandwiches, and bowls of your favorite salty snacks are always good options.

ROYAL COOKIE PARTY GAMES

There's nothing like a good game to get the party going! Here are a few games to try at your next gathering!

GUESS THE COOKIE Prepare several different cookies. Blindfold one princess at a time, then give her small bites of each cookie. The challenge is to guess the cookie flavor. Whoever gets the most correct answers wins royal favor—and a special treat!

COOKIE RACE Bake small cookies for this party game. Give each princess a spoon on which to balance a cookie and let the race begin. The first one to the finish line who doesn't drop their cookie wins!

ROYAL COOKIE TRIVIA Have the princesses form pairs or teams and challenge them to a trivia contest using cookie-themed questions. Use your imagination when coming up with questions! You can also throw in some Princess questions here, too, for extra royal fun.

PRINCESS GUESS WHO How well do your cookie party participants know their princesses? Find out with this fun guessing game. Have one Princess Cookie Party participant draw a princess name from a container. Then that participant must describe the Princess while the others guess who it is. Remember, no names in the description!

PRINCESS BINGO Create bingo boards using Princess names or related objects and corresponding slips of paper with the names or object words. Put the folded slips of paper in a bowl and select them, having Princess Cookie Party participants mark them off on their boards until someone gets a bingo! Have a special prize ready, like a tiara or coloring book, for the lucky winner. This game can be played a few times.

ROYAL TREASURE HUNT For this, you will need a treasure chest (or box) that can be filled with goodie bags or other treasures and trinkets and then hidden. Once the royal treasure chest is prepared, hide it in a hard-to-find location. Then create clues that will lead party guests from one to another until they find the treasure. Make sure the clues are age appropriate but also challenging.

ROYAL PARTY PUNCH

8 SERVINGS (ABOUT 11/2 CUPS EACH)

Even Princesses need a punch break! Sweet, tart and refreshing, this Royal Party Punch is a delightful addition to any party.

2 cups cranberry juice
2 cups pineapple juice
One 16-ounce can frozen lemonade
One 10-ounce package frozen strawberries
4 cups ginger ale
1 lime, thinly sliced

In a large pitcher or punch bowl, stir together the cranberry juice, pineapple juice, frozen lemonade, and frozen strawberries. Let sit for 10 minutes and stir again.

Just before serving, top the punch with ginger ale and lime slices.

THEMED MENUS

Use this guide to choose the perfect cookies for your Princess party, whatever the theme!

ADVENTURER PARTY

Wave Cookies (Moana)

Dragon Fruit Cheesecake Bars (Raya)

Warrior Bacon Double Chocolate Cookies (Merida)

Dark Side of the Moon Double Chocolate Cookies (Mulan)

FLOWER PARTY

Magnolia Blossom Cookies (Mulan)

Orange Blossom Sesame Chocolate Chip Cookies (Jasmine)

Party Like a Princess Frosted Soft Sugar Cookies

ROYAL COOKIE PARTY

Tiara Cookies (Aurora)

Dress Cookies (Belle)

Meringue Princess Wands

Royal Ball Tuiles (Cinderella)

ARTS AND CRAFTS PARTY

Nameplate Cookies

Sprinkle Cookies (Jasmine)

Bookish Brownie Bars (Belle)

FALL INTO AUTUMN PARTY

Carriage Pumpkin Chocolate Chip Cookies (Cinderella)

Iced Apple Cider Cookies (Snow White)

Ginger Molasses Cookies (Rapunzel)

Cornbread Cookies (Pocahontas)

COZY WINTER PARTY

Red Velvet Chocolate Chip Cookies (Belle)

Snowball Cookies (Belle)

Tuk Tuk Brown Sugar Oatmeal Cookies (Raya)

Scottish Shortbread (Merida)

LOVE IS IN THE AIR PARTY

Lost Shoe Cookies (Cinderella)

Evangeline's Sparkling Cinnamon Sugar Cookies (Tiana)

True Love's Kiss Cookies (Aurora)

Part of Your World Thumbprint Cookies (Ariel)

PRINCESS MAGIC PARTY

Meringue Princess Wands

Lantern Cookies (Rapunzel)

Magic Bars (Merida)

Heart of Te Fiti Cookies (Moana)

SUMMER FUN PARTY

Blueberry Beignets (Tiana)

Strawberry Rosewater White Chocolate Cookies (Aurora)

Starfish Cookies (Ariel)

Coconut Chocolate Chip Cookies (Moana)

CHAPTER ONE

CUTOUT COOKIES

TIARA COOKIES

PRINCESS: AURORA • YIELD: 24 COOKIES

For the first sixteen years of her life, Aurora isn't aware that she's a princess. After all, she has grown up with her three aunts in a cottage, not in a castle. She also doesn't know that her aunts are fairies with magical powers. She's in for quite a surprise when she turns sixteen and learns her true identity. These cookies celebrate Aurora's birthday and the tiara she receives when she finally returns to the castle.

FOR THE DOUGH

1½ cups confectioners' sugar

1 cup unsalted butter, softened

2 teaspoons pure vanilla extract

1 large egg

2½ cups all-purpose flour

2 teaspoons baking powder

FOR THE ICING

4 cups confectioners' sugar

3 tablespoons meringue powder

½ cup water, plus more as needed

Pink gel food coloring

Pink sanding sugar

SPECIAL EQUIPMENT

Tiara-shaped cookie cutter (3 to 4 inches wide)

TO MAKE THE COOKIES: In the bowl of a stand mixer fitted with the paddle attachment, combine the confectioners' sugar, butter, vanilla extract, and egg. Beat the ingredients together on the lowest speed until smooth, about 2 minutes. Add the flour and baking powder and mix together on low until combined, about 1 minute. Scrape down the sides of the bowl and mix for about 30 seconds more.

Cover the bowl with plastic wrap and chill in the refrigerator for at least 2 hours.

Preheat the oven to 375°F. Line a baking sheet with parchment paper.

On a floured work surface, use a floured rolling pin to roll out half the cookie dough to ¼ inch thick. Use the tiara-shaped cookie cutter to cut out the cookies. Carefully transfer them to the prepared baking sheet, leaving about 1½ inches between cookies.

Bake for 9 to 10 minutes, until the edges of the cookies are golden brown.

Remove from the oven and transfer the cookies to a cooling rack.

Repeat for the remaining dough.

Let cool completely before icing.

TO MAKE THE ICING: In the bowl of a stand mixer fitted with the whisk attachment, sift together the confectioners' sugar and meringue powder. Add the water a little at a time and mix on low for 1 minute, pausing to scrape down the sides of the bowl. Increase the speed to medium-high and whip until the icing is white, glossy, and smooth, about 1½ to 2 minutes.

If the icing drizzles off the whisk and smooths out slightly, it's ready to use. If not, add 1 tablespoon of water and run on medium-high for 30 seconds more. Continue, 1 tablespoon at a time, until the desired consistency is achieved.

Place about ¾ cup of the icing in a piping bag, securing the open end of the bag with a rubber band.

Add the pink food coloring, a little at a time, to the remaining icing and mix well to combine until the desired color is achieved. Transfer the pink icing to another piping bag and secure the open end with a rubber band.

TO DECORATE THE COOKIES: Carefully snip the end of the piping bag containing the pink icing. Pipe the outline of a tiara onto each cookie, then flood the center with icing. Use a toothpick to nudge the icing to a smooth covering. Continue until all the cookies have been decorated in pink.

Let the cookies stand for 30 minutes until the icing is firm.

Snip the end of the piping bag containing the white icing and outline the tiara, leaving a thin pink rim around the outside. Pipe white jewels on the points of the tiara. Use the remaining pink icing to pipe additional details, such as swirls and lines, on the tiara. Continue until all the cookies are decorated. Sprinkle with sanding sugar.

Let the icing harden completely before storing the cookies. Store in an airtight container at room temperature for up to 1 week.

DRESS COOKIES

PRINCESS: BELLE • YIELD: 18 COOKIES

Ever the compassionate and gentle one, Belle sees beyond Beast's tough, furry exterior to the soft heart inside. During her time in Beast's castle, she begins to enjoy his company while also making friends with Lumière, Cogsworth, Mrs. Potts, Chip, and others! Then one magical evening, wearing her signature off-the-shoulder yellow dress, she and Beast dance the night away. This cookie is inspired by that perfect scene and Belle's perfect dress.

FOR THE DOUGH

1½ cups confectioners' sugar

1 cup unsalted butter, softened

2 teaspoons pure vanilla extract

1 large egg

2½ cups all-purpose flour

2 teaspoons baking powder

FOR THE ICING

4 cups confectioners' sugar

3 tablespoons meringue powder

½ cup water, plus more as needed

Yellow gel food coloring

Red icing

SPECIAL EQUIPMENT

Dress-shaped cookie cutter (3 to 4 inches tall)

TO MAKE THE COOKIES: In the bowl of a stand mixer fitted with the paddle attachment, combine the confectioners' sugar, butter, vanilla extract, and egg. Beat the ingredients together on the lowest speed until smooth, about 2 minutes. Add the flour and baking powder and mix again on low to combine, about 1 minute. Scrape down the sides of the bowl and mix briefly, about 30 seconds.

Cover the bowl with plastic wrap and chill in the refrigerator for at least 2 hours.

Preheat the oven to 375°F. Line a baking sheet with parchment paper.

On a floured work surface, use a floured rolling pin to roll out half the cookie dough to ¼ inch thick. Use the dress-shaped cookie cutter to cut cookies from the dough. Carefully transfer them to the prepared baking sheet, leaving about 1½ inches between cookies.

Bake for 9 to 10 minutes, until the edges of the cookies are golden brown.

Remove from the oven and transfer the cookies to a cooling rack.

Repeat for the remaining dough.

Let cool completely before icing.

TO MAKE THE ICING: In the bowl of a stand mixer fitted with the whisk attachment, sift together the confectioners' sugar and meringue powder. Add the water a little at a time and mix on low for 1 minute, pausing to scrape down the sides of the bowl. Increase the speed to medium-high and whip until the icing is white, glossy, and smooth, about 1½ to 2 minutes.

Once the icing drizzles off the whisk and smooths out slightly, it's ready to use. If not, add 1 tablespoon of water and run on medium-high for 30 seconds more. Continue, 1 tablespoon at a time, until the desired consistency is achieved.

Add yellow food coloring to the icing and mix well. Add food coloring, mixing after each addition, until a gold color is achieved. Transfer to a piping bag and secure the open end with a rubber band, reserving about ¾ cup of icing.

Add food coloring to the reserved icing to make a darker yellow. Transfer to a piping bag and secure the open end with a rubber band.

TO DECORATE THE COOKIES: Snip the end of the piping bag with light yellow icing, cutting a small opening. Pipe an outline of a dress with an off-the-shoulder neckline on each cookie, then flood the center with icing. Use a toothpick to nudge the icing to a smooth covering. Continue until all the cookies are decorated.

Let the cookies stand for 30 minutes until the icing is firm.

Snip the end of the piping bag containing the dark yellow icing, cutting a small opening. Use the dark yellow icing to pipe the outline of an elongated bow-tie shape across the top of the dress. Add ruffles to the skirt using the dark yellow icing, creating a gathered look on the skirt from top to bottom. Continue until all the cookies are decorated. Pipe a small rose detail with red icing.

Let the icing harden completely before storing the cookies. Store in an airtight container at room temperature for up to 1 week.

LOST SHOE COOKIES

PRINCESS: CINDERELLA • YIELD: 24 COOKIES

Do you hear that? It's the sound of the clock striking midnight! No one knows better than Cinderella what that means: It's time to sprint to the pumpkin carriage before the spell wears off. She doesn't even have time to go back for her glass slipper when she loses it on the stairs. Luckily, though, that shoe brings her love back to her in the end! These delicious and fashionable cookies are an ode to the shoe that brought true love right to Cinderella's feet.

FOR THE DOUGH

1½ cups confectioners' sugar

1 cup unsalted butter, softened

2 teaspoons pure vanilla extract

1 large egg

2½ cups all-purpose flour

2 teaspoons baking powder

FOR THE ICING

4 cups confectioners' sugar

3 tablespoons meringue powder

½ cup water, plus more as needed

Blue gel food coloring

24 pearl sprinkles (optional)

SPECIAL EQUIPMENT

Shoe-shaped cookie cutter (3 to 4 inches long)

TO MAKE THE COOKIES: In the bowl of a stand mixer fitted with the paddle attachment, combine the confectioners' sugar, butter, vanilla extract, and egg. Beat the ingredients together on the lowest speed until smooth, about 2 minutes. Add the flour and baking powder and mix again on low to combine, about 1 minute. Scrape down the sides of the bowl and mix briefly, about 30 seconds.

Cover the bowl with plastic wrap and chill in the refrigerator for at least 2 hours.

Preheat the oven to 375°F. Line a baking sheet with parchment paper.

On a floured work surface, use a floured rolling pin to roll out half the cookie dough to ¼ inch thick. Use the shoe cookie cutter to cut out the cookies. Carefully transfer them to the prepared baking sheet, leaving about 1½ inches between cookies.

Bake for 9 to 10 minutes, until the edges of the cookies are golden brown.

Remove from the oven and transfer the cookies to a cooling rack.

Repeat for the remaining dough.

Let cool completely before icing.

TO MAKE THE ICING: In the bowl of a stand mixer fitted with the whisk attachment, sift together the confectioners' sugar and meringue powder. Add the water a little at a time and mix on low for 1 minute, pausing to scrape down the sides of the bowl. Increase the speed to medium-high and whip until the icing is white, glossy, and smooth, about 1½ to 2 minutes.

If the icing drizzles off the whisk and smooths out slightly, it's ready to use. If not, add 1 tablespoon of water and run on medium-high for 30 seconds more. Continue, 1 tablespoon at a time, until the desired consistency is achieved.

Remove about ¾ cup of icing from the stand mixer to a piping bag, securing the open end with a rubber band.

Add blue food coloring to the remaining icing and mix well to combine. Add food coloring, mixing after each addition, until a light blue color is achieved. Transfer to a piping bag and secure the open end with a rubber band.

TO DECORATE THE COOKIES: Brush the top (inside) of shoe with silver edible glitter. Snip the end of the blue piping bag, cutting a small opening. Pipe an outline of the shoe onto each cookie, then flood the center with icing. Use a toothpick to nudge the icing to a smooth covering. Continue until all the cookies have been decorated in blue.

Let the cookies stand for 30 minutes, until the icing is firm.

Pipe a blue bow and add a single pearl, if using.

Let the icing harden completely before storing the cookies. Store in an airtight container at room temperature for up to 1 week.

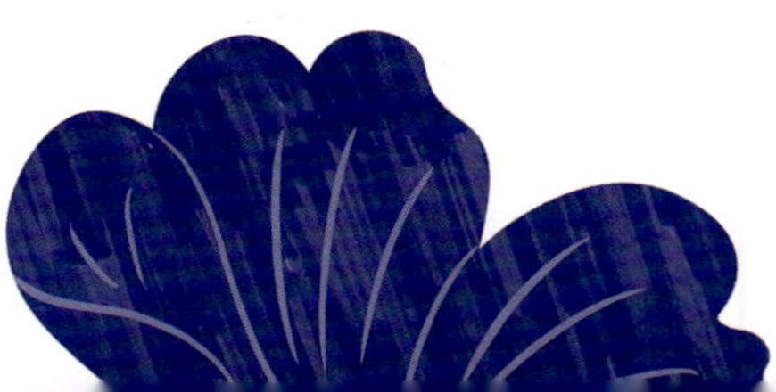

LANTERN COOKIES

PRINCESS: RAPUNZEL • YIELD: 18 COOKIES

Rapunzel always looks forward to that one evening each year when glowing lights float into the sky. Little does she know that the lights are released to honor the lost princess, and she is the princess they are lit for! The lanterns symbolize hope and the never-ending belief that someday the lost princess will find her way home. These cookies are as beautiful as they are tasty—and the perfect treat to share with family.

FOR THE DOUGH

1½ cups confectioners' sugar

1 cup unsalted butter, softened

2 teaspoons pure vanilla extract

1 large egg

2½ cups all-purpose flour

2 teaspoons baking powder

FOR THE ICING

4 cups confectioners' sugar

3 tablespoons meringue powder

½ cup water, plus more as needed

Yellow gel food coloring

Pink gel food coloring

White sanding sugar

SPECIAL EQUIPMENT

Rectangular or lantern cookie cutter (3 to 4 inches long)

TO MAKE THE COOKIES: In the bowl of a stand mixer fitted with the paddle attachment, combine the confectioners' sugar, butter, vanilla extract, and egg. Beat on the lowest speed until the mixture is smooth, about 2 minutes. Add the flour and baking powder and mix again on low to combine, about 1 minute. Scrape down the sides of the bowl and mix briefly, about 30 seconds.

Cover the bowl with plastic wrap and chill in the refrigerator for at least 2 hours.

Preheat the oven to 375°F. Line a baking sheet with parchment paper.

On a floured work surface, use a floured rolling pin to roll out half the cookie dough to ¼ inch thick. Use the cookie cutter to cut out the cookies. Transfer carefully to the prepared baking sheet. Continue, leaving about 1½ inches between the cookies, until the baking sheet is filled.

Bake for 9 to 10 minutes, until the edges of the cookies are golden brown.

Remove the baking sheet from the oven and transfer the cookies to a cooling rack.

Repeat for the remaining dough.

Let cool completely before icing.

TO MAKE THE ICING: In the bowl of a stand mixer fitted with the whisk attachment, sift together the confectioners' sugar and meringue powder. Add the water a little at a time and mix on low for 1 minute, pausing to scrape down the sides of the bowl. Increase the speed to medium-high and whip until the icing is white, glossy, and smooth, about 1½ to 2 minutes.

If the icing drizzles off the whisk and smooths out slightly, it's ready to use. If not, add 1 tablespoon of water and run on medium-high for 30 seconds to incorporate. Continue, 1 tablespoon at a time, until the desired consistency is achieved.

Remove about 1⅓ cups of icing from the stand mixer to a piping bag, securing the open end with a rubber band.

Divide the remaining icing between 2 bowls. Add pink food coloring to one bowl and mix well to combine. Add yellow food coloring to the other bowl, mixing well to combine. Add more food coloring, if needed, to achieve the desired colors. Transfer each icing to a piping bag and secure the open end with a rubber band.

TO DECORATE THE COOKIES: Snip the end of the piping bag containing the white icing, cutting a small opening. Pipe an outline of the cookie, then flood the center with icing. Use a toothpick to nudge the icing to a smooth covering. Pipe yellow and pink circles in the center. Use toothpick to pull the icing into a sunburst shape. Repeat for the remaining cookies.

Let the cookies stand for 30 minutes, until the icing is firm.

Sprinkle the center with sanding sugar. Using the yellow icing, pipe an outline around the cookie. Repeat for the remaining cookies.

Let the icing harden completely before storing the cookies. Store in an airtight container at room temperature for up to 1 week.

STARFISH COOKIES

PRINCESS: ARIEL • YIELD: 18 COOKIES

Princess Ariel is fascinated by life outside the ocean, up where people walk and run all day. Despite her longing, she can't deny that her sea kingdom is filled with amazing marine life of all kinds that keep her entertained. From her best friend, Flounder—a tropical fish—to dancing starfish, life under the sea can be very exciting, even if she'd rather be playing in the sun. Whip up a batch of these starfish cookies for your next ocean-themed party!

FOR THE DOUGH

1½ cups confectioners' sugar

1 cup unsalted butter, softened

2 teaspoons pure vanilla extract

1 large egg

2½ cups all-purpose flour

2 teaspoons baking powder

FOR THE ICING

4 cups confectioners' sugar

3 tablespoons meringue powder

½ cup water, plus more as needed

Turquoise gel food coloring

SPECIAL EQUIPMENT

Starfish-shaped cookie cutter (3 to 4 inches wide)

TO MAKE THE COOKIES: In the bowl of a stand mixer fitted with the paddle attachment, combine the confectioners' sugar, butter, vanilla extract, and egg. Beat the ingredients together on the lowest speed until the mixture is smooth, about 2 minutes. Add the flour and baking powder and mix again on low to combine, about 1 minute. Scrape down the sides of the bowl and mix briefly, about 30 seconds.

Cover the bowl with plastic wrap and chill in the refrierator for at least 2 hours.

Preheat the oven to 375°F. Line a baking sheet with parchment paper.

On a floured work surface, use a floured rolling pin to roll out half the cookie dough to ¼ inch thick. Use the starfish cookie cutter to cut out the cookies. Transfer carefully to the prepared baking sheet. Continue, leaving about 1½ inches between the cookies, until the baking sheet is filled.

Bake for 9 to 10 minutes, until the edges of the cookies are golden brown.

Remove from the oven and transfer the cookies to a cooling rack.

Repeat for the remaining dough.

Let cool completely before icing.

TO MAKE THE ICING: In the bowl of a stand mixer fitted with the whisk attachment, sift together the confectioners' sugar and meringue powder. Add the water a little at a time and mix on low for 1 minute, pausing to scrape down the sides of the bowl. Increase the speed to medium-high and whip until the icing is white, glossy, and smooth, about 1½ to 2 minutes.

If the icing drizzles off the whisk and smooths out slightly, it's ready to use. If not, add 1 tablespoon of water and run on medium-high for 30 seconds to incorporate. Continue, 1 tablespoon at a time, until the desired consistency is achieved.

Remove ½ cup of icing from the stand mixer to a piping bag, securing the open end with a rubber band.

Add turquoise food coloring to the remaining icing and mix well to combine. Add food coloring, mixing after each addition, until a turquoise color is achieved. Transfer to a piping bag and secure the open end with a rubber band.

TO DECORATE THE COOKIES: Snip the end of the piping bag with turquoise icing, cutting a small opening. Pipe an outline of the starfish onto each cookie, then flood the center with icing. Use a toothpick to nudge the icing to a smooth covering. Continue until all the cookies are decorated in turquoise.

Let the cookies stand for 1 hour until the icing is firm.

Snip the end of the white piping bag and pipe small dots onto each starfish leg, as well as a large dot in the center. Continue until all the cookies are decorated.

Let the icing harden completely before storing the cookies. Store in an airtight container at room temperature for up to 1 week.

NAMEPLATE COOKIES

YIELD: 18 COOKIES

Who will you be celebrating at your Disney Princess Cookie Party? These clever cookies can be used for any Princess at all—including the ones in your home. Get creative and make something beautiful! And remember, little ones might need a bit of extra royal help to write their own names with icing! Demonstrate how to write with icing on a plate so kids can see how it's done before they try.

FOR THE DOUGH

1½ cups confectioners' sugar

1 cup unsalted butter, softened

2 teaspoons pure vanilla extract

1 large egg

2½ cups all-purpose flour

2 teaspoons baking powder

FOR THE ICING

4 cups confectioners' sugar

3 tablespoons meringue powder

½ cup water, plus more as needed

Gel food coloring (colors of your choice)

SPECIAL EQUIPMENT

Nameplate-shaped cookie cutter (3 to 4 inches wide)

TO MAKE THE COOKIES: In the bowl of a stand mixer fitted with the paddle attachment, combine the confectioners' sugar, butter, vanilla extract, and egg. Beat the ingredients together on the lowest speed until smooth, about 2 minutes. Add the flour and baking powder and mix on low to combine, about 1 minute. Scrape down the sides of the bowl and mix briefly, about 30 seconds.

Cover the bowl with plastic wrap and chill in the refrigerator for at least 2 hours.

Preheat the oven to 375°F. Line a baking sheet with parchment paper.

On a floured work surface, use a floured rolling pin to roll out half the cookie dough to ¼ inch thick. Use the tiara cookie cutter to cut out the cookies. Transfer carefully to the prepared baking sheet. Continue, leaving about 1½ inches between the cookies, until the baking sheet is filled.

Bake for 9 to 10 minutes, until the edges of the cookies are golden brown.

Remove from the oven and transfer the cookies to a cooling rack.

Repeat for the remaining dough.

Cool completely before icing.

TO MAKE THE ICING: In the bowl of a stand mixer fitted with the whisk attachment, sift together the confectioners' sugar and meringue powder. Add the water a little at a time and mix on low for 1 minute, pausing to scrape down the sides of the bowl. Increase the speed to medium-high and whip until the icing is white, glossy, and smooth, about 1½ to 2 minutes.

If the icing drizzles off the whisk and smooths out slightly, it's ready to use. If not, add 1 tablespoon of water and run on medium-high for 30 seconds to incorporate. Continue, 1 tablespoon at a time, until the desired consistency is achieved.

Add food coloring to the icing in the color of your choice and mix well to combine. Add food coloring, mixing after each addition, until the desired color is achieved. Transfer to a piping bag and secure the open end with a rubber band.

TO DECORATE THE COOKIES: Snip the end of the piping bag, cutting a small opening. Pipe an outline of the nameplate onto each cookie, then flood the center with icing. Use a toothpick to nudge the icing to a smooth covering. Continue until all the cookies are covered in icing.

Let the cookies stand for 1 to 2 hours until the icing is firm.

Pipe on the name. Use the remaining icing to pipe additional details, as desired. Continue until all the cookies are decorated.

Let the icing harden completely before storing the cookies. Store in an airtight container at room temperature for up to 1 week.

Merida
Tiana
Belle
Moana

MAGNOLIA BLOSSOM COOKIES

PRINCESS: MULAN • YIELD: 18 COOKIES

Strong-willed Mulan has a fighting spirit that helps her stay calm and collected when she takes her father's place in battle while disguised as a man. As Ping, her alias, she shows her strength and cleverness, learning to sword fight, solving puzzles, and eventually defeating Shan Yu, leader of the Huns. Mulan's name translates to "magnolia," a flower native to China. These delicate flowers symbolize strength, nobility, and resilience, which sounds a lot like our favorite warrior!

FOR THE DOUGH

1½ cups confectioners' sugar

1 cup unsalted butter, softened

2 teaspoons pure vanilla extract

1 large egg

2½ cups all-purpose flour

2 teaspoons baking powder

FOR THE ICING

4 cups confectioners' sugar

3 tablespoons meringue powder

½ cup water, plus more as needed

Pink gel food coloring

Green gel food coloring

FOR THE DECORATION

White granulated sugar

SPECIAL EQUIPMENT

Flower-shaped cookie cutter (3 to 4 inches wide)

TO MAKE THE COOKIES: In the bowl of a stand mixer fitted with the paddle attachment, combine the confectioners' sugar, butter, vanilla extract, and egg. Beat the ingredients together on the lowest speed until smooth, about 2 minutes. Add the flour and baking powder and mix again on low to combine, about 1 minute. Scrape down the sides of the bowl and mix briefly, about 30 seconds.

Cover the bowl with plastic wrap and chill in the refrigerator for at least 2 hours.

Preheat the oven to 375°F. Line a baking sheet with parchment paper.

On a floured work surface, use a floured rolling pin to roll out half of the cookie dough to ¼ inch thick. Use the flower cookie cutter to cut out the cookies. Transfer carefully to the prepared baking sheet. Continue, leaving about 1½ inches between the cookies, until the baking sheet is filled.

Bake for 9 to 10 minutes, until the edges of the cookies are golden brown.

Remove from the oven and transfer the cookies to a cooling rack.

Repeat for the remaining dough.

Cool completely before icing.

TO MAKE THE ICING: In the bowl of a stand mixer fitted with the whisk attachment, sift together the confectioners' sugar and meringue powder. Add the water a little at a time and mix on low for 1 minute, pausing to scrape down the sides of the bowl. Increase the speed to medium-high and whip until the icing is white, glossy, and smooth, about 1½ to 2 minutes.

If the icing drizzles off the whisk and smooths out slightly, it's ready to use. If not, add 1 tablespoon of water and run on medium-high for 30 seconds to incorporate. Continue, 1 tablespoon at a time, until the desired consistency is achieved.

Remove about 1½ cups of icing from the stand mixer to a piping bag, securing the open end with a rubber band.

Remove ½ cup of icing and stir in the green food coloring. Add to a piping bag, securing the open end with a rubber band. Add pink food coloring to the remaining icing and mix well to combine. Add food coloring, mixing after each addition, until a pink color is achieved. Transfer to a piping bag and secure the open end with a rubber band.

TO DECORATE THE COOKIES: Snip the end of the piping bag with white icing, cutting a small opening. Pipe an outline of the flower onto each cookie, then lightly flood the center with icing. Use a toothpick to nudge the icing to a smooth covering. Continue until all the cookies are decorated in white. Pipe pink onto the center and use a toothpick to blend it into the white icing.

Let the cookies stand for 30 minutes, until the icing is firm. Using white icing, pipe the outlines of the petals.

Pipe pink dots onto the center of the cookie. Flood the leaves with green icing. Continue until all the cookies are decorated. Sprinkle with granulated sugar.

Let the icing harden completely before storing. Store in an airtight container at room temperature for up to 1 week.

WAVE COOKIES

PRINCESS: MOANA • YIELD: 18 COOKIES

The ocean takes on a life of its own in Moana's world, its watery depth hiding secrets and its waves revealing them. Moana is fascinated by the ocean, but she resists its pull, focusing on being a good leader in her village instead until a curse threatens their island. Moana's relationship with the ocean runs deep, and this respect she has for it helps her on her journey. Celebrate Moana's adventurous spirit with these simple, delicious cutout wave cookies.

FOR THE DOUGH

1½ cups confectioners' sugar

1 cup unsalted butter, softened

2 teaspoons pure vanilla extract

1 large egg

2½ cups all-purpose flour

2 teaspoons baking powder

FOR THE ICING

4 cups confectioners' sugar

3 tablespoons meringue powder

½ cup water, plus more as needed

Blue gel food coloring

SPECIAL EQUIPMENT

Round cookie cutter (3 to 4 inches in diameter)

TO MAKE THE COOKIES: In the bowl of a stand mixer fitted with the paddle attachment, combine the confectioners' sugar, butter, vanilla extract, and egg. Beat the ingredients together on the lowest speed until smooth, about 2 minutes. Add the flour and baking powder and mix again on low to combine, about 1 minute. Scrape down the sides of the bowl and mix briefly, about 30 seconds.

Cover the bowl with plastic wrap and chill in the refrigerator for at least 2 hours.

Preheat the oven to 375°F. Line a baking sheet with parchment paper.

On a floured work surface, use a floured rolling pin to roll out half the cookie dough to ¼ inch thick. Use the cookie cutter to cut out the cookies. Transfer carefully to the prepared baking sheet. Continue, leaving about 1½ inches between the cookies, until the baking sheet is filled.

Bake for 9 to 10 minutes, until the edges of the cookies are golden brown.

Remove from the oven and transfer the cookies to a cooling rack.

Repeat for the remaining dough.

Cool completely before icing.

TO MAKE THE ICING: In the bowl of a stand mixer fitted with the whisk attachment, sift together the confectioners' sugar and meringue powder. Add the water, and mix on low for 1 minute, pausing to scrape down the sides of the bowl. Increase the speed to medium-high and whip until the icing is white, glossy, and smooth, about 1½ to 2 minutes.

If the icing drizzles off the whisk and smooths out slightly, it's ready to use. If not, add 1 tablespoon of water and run on medium-high for 30 seconds to incorporate. Continue, 1 tablespoon at a time, until the desired consistency is achieved.

Remove about 1½ cups of icing from the stand mixer to a piping bag, securing the open end with a rubber band.

Add food coloring to the remaining icing, mixing after each addition, until the desired color of blue is achieved. Mix well to combine. Transfer to a piping bag and secure the open end with a rubber band.

TO DECORATE THE COOKIES: Snip the end of the piping bag with white icing, cutting a small opening. Pipe the outline of the circle onto each cookie, then flood the center with icing. Use a toothpick to nudge the icing to a smooth covering. Continue until all the cookies are decorated in white icing. Use the blue icing to draw a wave outline onto each cookie. You can create two different shades of blue icing, if desired, by adding more food coloring to one. Use a toothpick to swirl the color together with the white. Continue until all the cookies are decorated.

Let the icing harden completely before storing the cookies. Store in an airtight container at room temperature for up to 1 week.

CHAPTER TWO

CHIP COOKIES

WHITE CHOCOLATE CHIP WALNUT COOKIE SKILLET

PRINCESS: RAPUNZEL • YIELD: 6 SERVINGS

Buttery, sweet, and a little gooey, this White Chocolate Chip Walnut Cookie Skillet is easy to whip up and ideal for sharing. It tastes best served warm from the oven alongside a scoop of vanilla ice cream or whipped cream. This treat is made in a cast-iron skillet, not unlike the one Rapunzel uses to defend herself when Flynn Rider breaks into her tower home!

½ cup unsalted butter, plus 1 teaspoon for greasing
½ cup dark brown sugar
¼ cup sugar
1 large egg
1 teaspoon pure vanilla extract
1¼ cups all-purpose flour
½ teaspoon kosher salt
1 teaspoon baking soda
1 cup white chocolate chips
1 cup chopped walnuts
Vanilla ice cream or whipped cream (optional)

Preheat the oven to 350°F. Grease an 9- or 10-inch cast-iron skillet with 1 teaspoon of butter, rubbing it thoroughly over the bottom and sides of the pan.

In a small saucepan, melt the butter. Pour the melted butter into a large mixing bowl and stir in the brown sugar and sugar. Add the egg and vanilla extract and stir well to combine.

In a small bowl, sift together the flour, salt, and baking soda. Add the flour mixture to the wet ingredients and mix well. Add the white chocolate chips and walnuts and stir to combine.

Use a rubber spatula to transfer the cookie dough into the prepared cast-iron skillet, then press it into an even layer.

Bake for 30 to 35 minutes. Baking for 30 minutes will produce a cookie with a gooey center; for a more set center, bake for 35 minutes.

Serve warm with a scoop of vanilla ice cream or whipped cream.

For best results, remove leftovers from the pan while still warm. Store in an airtight container in the refrigerator for up to 5 days.

WARRIOR BACON DOUBLE CHOCOLATE COOKIES

PRINCESS: MERIDA • YIELD: 36 COOKIES

While Merida's mother would like her to be a well-mannered princess, Merida would rather be in the woods, on her horse, or practicing archery. Her skills, much like these cookies, pack quite the surprise for those who underestimate her. Sweet, buttery chocolate chip cookies meet salty, savory bacon—it's the perfect unlikely pairing!

- 1 cup unsalted butter, softened
- 1¼ cups light brown sugar
- 1 teaspoon pure vanilla extract
- 2 large eggs
- 2¼ cups all-purpose flour
- 1 teaspoon baking soda
- 1 teaspoon kosher salt
- 2 cups dark chocolate chips
- 9 slices bacon, fried and chopped, reserving 1 slice
- 4 ounces milk chocolate

Preheat the oven to 375°F. Line a nonstick baking sheet with parchment paper.

In the bowl of a stand mixer fitted with the paddle attachment, cream the butter and brown sugar. Beat for about 30 seconds at low speed. Increase the speed to medium and beat for 2 minutes more, or until the mixture is light and fluffy.

Add the vanilla extract and eggs to the bowl. Beat on medium until all the ingredients are thoroughly combined.

In a large bowl, sift together the flour, baking soda, and salt. With the mixer running on low, add the flour mixture a little at a time to the bowl until just combined. Add the chocolate chips and 8 slices of the chopped bacon. Mix briefly to combine.

Using a medium cookie scoop, drop the dough in balls onto the prepared baking sheet. Bake for 9 to 11 minutes, or until the cookies are golden brown on the edges and the center is baked. Remove from the oven and let stand for 2 minutes before transferring to a cooling rack to cool completely.

Place the cooled cookies on a baking sheet lined with wax paper (it's okay if they touch).

Crumble the milk chocolate into a microwave-safe bowl. Heat for 30 seconds on high and then stir. Heat for an additional 30 seconds and stir again. The chocolate should be melted. Use a spoon to drizzle it over the cookies.

Crumble the remaining slice of bacon and sprinkle it on top. These cookies are delightful served warm!

Store in an airtight container in the refrigerator for up to 5 days.

COCONUT CHOCOLATE CHIP COOKIES

PRINCESS: MOANA • YIELD: 24 COOKIES

One of the biggest resources on Moana's home island is the coconut. This versatile fruit is eaten, of course, but it is also used to create tools such as fishing nets. These tropical cookies are perfect for coconut lovers. With the familiar texture of shredded coconut and dotted with chocolate, they are delicious straight from the oven and (if possible) even tastier the next day.

1¼ cups all-purpose flour
1 teaspoon baking soda
¼ teaspoon baking powder
½ teaspoon kosher salt
½ cup unsalted butter, softened
½ cup packed light brown sugar
½ cup sugar
1 large egg
1½ teaspoons pure vanilla extract
½ teaspoon coconut extract
2 cups semisweet chocolate chips
1 cup dried unsweetened coconut flakes

Preheat the oven to 350°F. Line a baking sheet with parchment paper.

In a large bowl, sift together the flour, baking soda, baking powder, and salt. Set aside.

In the bowl of a stand mixer fitted with the paddle attachment, cream together the butter, brown sugar, and sugar, first on low and then on medium speed, for a total of about 2 minutes, or until the mixture becomes light and fluffy. Add the egg, vanilla extract, and coconut extract to the bowl and mix on medium until combined, about 30 seconds to 1 minute.

With the mixer running on its lowest speed, add the flour mixture a little at a time until just combined. Add the chocolate chips and coconut flakes and mix until just combined.

Using a medium cookie scoop, scoop the cookie dough onto the prepared baking sheet, leaving about 2 inches between each mound of dough.

Bake the cookies for 10 to 13 minutes, or until they are golden brown on the edges. Remove from the oven and cool for 3 minutes on the baking sheet before transferring to a cooling rack.

Store in an airtight container at room temperature for up to 1 week.

HARVEST MULTIGRAIN CHOCOLATE CHIP COOKIES

PRINCESS: POCAHONTAS • YIELD: 24 COOKIES

Pocahontas is bold and free spirited, and she spends her days forging deep connections with the natural world around her. Pocahontas lives at a time when grains, such as oats and corn, are essential to her tribe's diet. These hearty, chocolaty cookies celebrate grains and seeds in a delicious, irresistible form. And Meeko, Pocahontas's mischievous, seed-loving raccoon friend, would very much approve.

½ cup unsalted butter, softened

½ cup packed light brown sugar

¼ cup sugar

1 teaspoon pure vanilla extract

1 large egg

1 cup whole wheat flour

½ cup old-fashioned rolled oats (not instant)

½ cup sunflower seeds

½ teaspoon kosher salt

1 teaspoon baking soda

2 cups semisweet chocolate chips

Preheat the oven to 375°F. Line a baking sheet with parchment paper.

Combine the butter, brown sugar, and sugar in the bowl of a stand mixer fitted with the paddle attachment. Beat on medium speed until light and fluffy, about 2 minutes. Add the vanilla extract and egg and beat until combined, about 1 minute.

In a large bowl, mix together the flour, oats, sunflower seeds, salt, and baking soda.

With the stand mixer running at its lowest speed, add the flour mixture to the butter mixture 1 scoop at a time, until just incorporated. Stir in the chocolate chips.

Using a medium cookie scoop, scoop the cookie dough onto the baking sheet, leaving about 2 inches between the mounds of dough.

Bake the cookies for 10 to 12 minutes, or until they are golden brown on the edges. Remove from the oven and cool on the baking sheet for 3 minutes before transferring to a cooling rack to cool completely.

Store in an airtight container at room temperature for up to 1 week.

ORANGE BLOSSOM SESAME CHOCOLATE CHIP COOKIES

PRINCESS: JASMINE • YIELD: 24 COOKIES

You've never had cookies like these! Don't be fooled by the fruit in the name! Orange blossom water gives these unique cookies a pleasant floral flavor, while the chocolate chips add extra sweetness and the sesame seeds bring a unique texture.

¾ cup unsalted butter, softened
1 cup packed light brown sugar
1 teaspoon orange blossom water
2 large eggs
1½ cups all-purpose flour
½ teaspoon kosher salt
¼ teaspoon baking powder
½ cup mini semisweet chocolate chips
¼ cup sesame seeds

Preheat the oven to 375°F. Line 2 baking sheets with parchment paper.

In the bowl of a stand mixer fitted with the paddle attachment, beat together the butter and brown sugar until fluffy, about 2 minutes. Add the orange blossom water and eggs and beat on medium-low until all the ingredients are fully incorporated, about 1 minute.

In a small bowl, sift together the flour, salt, and baking powder. With the mixer running on low, add the flour mixture to the wet ingredients a little at a time until incorporated.

Fold in the mini chocolate chips and sesame seeds.

Using a medium cookie scoop, scoop out balls of cookie dough and place them on the prepared baking sheets, leaving about 2 inches between the cookies.

Bake each batch of cookies for 8 to 10 minutes, or until golden brown at the edges and baked through. Remove from the oven and cool for 5 minutes on the baking sheet before transferring to a cooling rack to cool completely.

Store in an airtight container at room temperature for up to 5 days.

CARRIAGE PUMPKIN CHOCOLATE CHIP COOKIES

PRINCESS: CINDERELLA • YIELD: 24 COOKIES

We all remember the magical moment when Cinderella's pumpkin carriage whisks her away to the ball at the castle, where she meets her beloved prince. These cookies, rich with pumpkin flavor and dotted with dark chocolate, will whisk you away, too, with their sweet, nuanced flavor. As an added treat, they are easy to make and fun to share at your next Princess party!

2¼ cups all-purpose flour
½ teaspoon ground ginger
1 teaspoon ground cinnamon
1 teaspoon baking soda
1 teaspoon baking powder
½ teaspoon kosher salt
½ cup unsalted butter, softened
1¼ cups packed light brown sugar
1 cup pumpkin purée
1 egg
1 teaspoon pure vanilla extract
2 cups dark chocolate chips
Coarse gold sanding sugar

Preheat the oven to 350°F. Line a baking sheet with parchment paper.

In a medium bowl, sift together the flour, ginger, cinnamon, baking soda, baking powder, and salt. Set aside.

In the bowl of a stand mixer, or in a large bowl if using a handheld mixer, cream together the butter and brown sugar on medium speed until light and fluffy, about 2 minutes. Add the pumpkin purée, egg, and vanilla extract and beat until well combined, about 1 minute.

With the mixer running at its lowest speed, add the flour mixture to the wet ingredients a little at a time, until fully combined. Don't overmix. Add the chocolate chips and mix briefly to combine.

Using a medium cookie scoop, scoop mounds of cookie dough onto the baking sheet, leaving about 2 inches between cookies. Sprinkle with sanding sugar.

Bake for 10 to 15 minutes, or until slightly browned. Remove from the oven and transfer to a cooling rack to cool completely.

Store in an airtight container at room temperature for up to 5 days.

STRAWBERRY ROSEWATER WHITE CHOCOLATE COOKIES

PRINCESS: AURORA • YIELD: 24 COOKIES

Fragrant and sweet, these fruity cookies are delicate but bold, just like Aurora, the Princess with lips as red as a rose who is cursed by Maleficent to prick her finger on her sixteenth birthday and fall into a deep sleep. Here, strawberry meets rosewater—a light and floral flavor that is enhanced by the white chocolate chips—making these both decadent and light.

1¼ cups all-purpose flour
1 teaspoon baking powder
½ teaspoon salt
½ cup unsalted butter, softened
½ cup packed light brown sugar
½ cup sugar
1 large egg
1 teaspoon strawberry extract
1 teaspoon rosewater
¼ teaspoon pure vanilla extract
1 teaspoon red gel food coloring
2 cups white chocolate chips
Red sanding sugar

Preheat the oven to 350°F. Line a baking sheet with parchment paper.

In a medium mixing bowl, sift together the flour, baking powder, and salt. Set aside.

In the bowl of a stand mixer fitted with the paddle attachment, cream together the butter, brown sugar, and sugar, starting on low and then increasing the speed to medium. Beat for about 2 minutes, or until the mixture is light and fluffy. Add the egg, strawberry extract, rosewater, and vanilla extract. Beat for 1 minute.

With the mixer running at its lowest speed, add the flour mixture a little at a time until it is fully incorporated, about 1 minute. Add the white chocolate chips and mix briefly to combine.

Use a medium cookie scoop to scoop the cookie dough in mounds onto the prepared baking sheet, leaving about 2 inches between each cookie. Sprinkle with sanding sugar.

Bake for 10 to 12 minutes, or until the cookies are golden brown at the edges and dry on top.

Remove from the oven and let cool for 3 minutes before transferring the cookies to a cooling rack to cool completely.

Store in an airtight container at room temperature for up to 1 week.

RED VELVET CHOCOLATE CHIP COOKIES

PRINCESS: BELLE • YIELD: 24 COOKIES

Delicate white chocolate steals the show in this decadent treat. These Red Velvet Chocolate Chip Cookies are a sweet treat that's a perfect tribute to a book-loving Princess who finds an enchanted rose in Beast's west wing. Belle is so taken with the rose that she can't look away. Perhaps you should make a batch to enjoy while reading your favorite books!

1⅔ cups all-purpose flour
¼ cup unsweetened cocoa powder
1 teaspoon baking soda
½ teaspoon kosher salt
½ cup unsalted butter, softened
½ cup packed light brown sugar
½ cup sugar
1 large egg
1 teaspoon pure vanilla extract
1 teaspoon red gel food coloring
1 cup white chocolate chips

Preheat the oven to 350°F. Line a baking sheet with parchment paper.

In a medium mixing bowl, sift together the flour, cocoa powder, baking soda, and salt. Set aside.

In the bowl of a stand mixer fitted with the paddle attachment, cream together the butter, brown sugar, and sugar for about 2 minutes, or until light and fluffy. Start on low and increase to medium speed. Add the egg and vanilla extract and mix on medium-low until combined.

With the mixer running on its lowest setting, add the flour mixture a little at a time until fully incorporated. Add the red gel food coloring and mix briefly to combine. Add the white chocolate chips and mix to combine. Cover with plastic wrap and chill in the refrigerator for 30 minutes.

Use a medium cookie scoop to drop balls of dough onto the baking sheet, leaving about 3 inches between cookies.

Bake for 10 to 11 minutes, or until set. Remove from the oven and cool for 3 minutes before transferring to a cooling rack.

Store in an airtight container at room temperature for up to 1 week.

JAZZY CHOCOLATE CHIP COOKIE ICE CREAM SANDWICHES

PRINCESS: TIANA • YIELD: 4 SANDWICHES

One bite of these cookies and you'll feel the sweet music of New Orleans move your feet, just as Tiana and Prince Naveen do when they're cutting loose on stage at Tiana's Palace. A touch of oats gives these chocolate chip cookies a firmness that makes them ideal for ice cream sandwiches, while music note sprinkles capture the party vibe perfectly. If you can't find music note sprinkles, green, yellow, and purple sprinkles are perfect for a Mardi Gras celebration!

- ½ cup unsalted butter, softened
- ½ cup packed brown sugar
- ¼ cup sugar
- 1 large egg
- 1 teaspoon pure vanilla extract
- ½ cup mini chocolate chips
- 1 cup all-purpose flour
- ¼ cup old-fashioned rolled oats (not instant)
- ½ teaspoon baking soda
- ½ teaspoon kosher salt
- 2 cups vanilla ice cream
- Music note sprinkles or sprinkles of your choice

Preheat the oven to 375°F. Line a baking sheet with parchment paper.

In the bowl of a stand mixer fitted with the paddle attachment, cream together the butter, brown sugar, and sugar. Add the egg and vanilla extract and run on medium speed until the ingredients are fully combined, about 1 minute. Stir in the the chocolate chips.

In a large mixing bowl, sift together the flour, oats, baking soda, and salt with a wire whisk. With the stand mixer running on its lowest speed, add the flour mixture a little at a time until fully incorporated, about 1 minute.

Using a large cookie scoop (or 2 tablespoons), drop mounds of cookie dough onto the prepared baking sheet, leaving about 2 inches between each mound.

Bake for 8 to 10 minutes, until golden brown.

Remove from the oven and let cool for 2 minutes before transferring to a cooling rack. Repeat for the remaining dough. Freeze the cookies.

Soften the ice cream for 20 to 30 minutes before preparing the sandwiches. Divide it evenly among half of the cookies and place a scoop on top. Close with the remaining cookies, forming sandwiches and pressing to even out the ice cream. Roll the sandwiches in sprinkles.

Wrap each sandwich in plastic wrap and chill in the freezer for at least 30 minutes before serving.

Store in the freezer for up to 3 months.

WHISTLE WHILE YOU WORK CLASSIC CHOCOLATE CHIP COOKIES

PRINCESS: SNOW WHITE • YIELD: 36 COOKIES

These cookies are a classic, just like the very first Disney Princess, Snow White. Some might even call them the fairest chocolate chip cookie in all the land! This hard-working recipe gives you rich, buttery cookies with a perfect chocolate distribution that you'll keep coming back for. Serve with a big glass of milk for the ultimate classic treat.

- 1¼ cups unbleached all-purpose flour
- 1 teaspoon baking soda
- ½ teaspoon kosher salt
- ½ cup unsalted butter, softened
- ½ cup packed light brown sugar
- ½ cup sugar
- 1 large egg
- 1 teaspoon pure vanilla extract
- 2 cups milk chocolate chips

Preheat the oven to 350°F. Line a baking sheet with parchment paper.

In a large mixing bowl, add the flour, baking soda, and salt. Use a whisk to sift together. Set aside.

In the bowl of a stand mixer fitted with the paddle attachment, cream together the butter, brown sugar, and sugar. Beat on medium speed until smooth, about 2 minutes. With the mixer running on its lowest speed, add the egg and vanilla extract to the mixer. Slowly add the flour mixture, 1 spoonful at a time, until fully blended. Add the chocolate chips and beat until just combined.

Use a medium cookie scoop to drop the dough into even mounds on the prepared baking sheet, leaving about 2 inches between cookies.

Bake for 10 to 13 minutes, or until the cookies are lightly browned. Let cool for 5 minutes before transferring to a cooling rack to cool completely.

Store in an airtight container at room temperature for up to 1 week.

DARK SIDE OF THE MOON DOUBLE CHOCOLATE COOKIES

PRINCESS: MULAN • YIELD: 36 COOKIES

Love chocolate? Then these dark chocolate cookies with chocolate chips are perfect for you! They are rich and deeply flavored, with a lovely soft texture. There is something mysterious (like the dark side of the moon!) about these cookies, much like there is about Mulan, who disguises herself to become a warrior.

1 cup unsalted butter, softened

1 cup sugar

½ cup packed light brown sugar

2 large eggs

1 teaspoon pure vanilla extract

2 cups all-purpose flour

⅔ cup Dutch-processed cocoa powder

1 teaspoon baking soda

½ teaspoon kosher salt

2 cups dark chocolate chips

Preheat the oven to 350°F. Line a baking sheet with parchment paper.

In the bowl of a stand mixer fitted with the paddle attachment, add the butter, sugar, and brown sugar. Cream together on low, then on medium speed for about 2 minutes, or until light and fluffy. Add the eggs and vanilla extract to the bowl and beat into the butter mixture for about 1 minute, scraping down the sides of the bowl.

In a medium mixing bowl, sift together the flour, cocoa powder, baking soda, and salt. With the mixer running on low, add the flour mixture a little at a time until it is just incorporated.

Add the chocolate chips and mix briefly to combine.

Using a medium cookie scoop, drop mounds of cookie dough onto the prepared baking sheet, leaving about 2 inches between cookies. Bake for 10 to 12 minutes, or until the cookies look dry on top. Let cool for 3 minutes before transferring to a cooling rack to cool completely.

Store in an airtight container at room temperature for up to 1 week.

CHAPTER THREE

CLASSIC COOKIES

PARTY LIKE A PRINCESS FROSTED SOFT SUGAR COOKIES

YIELD: 24 COOKIES

Princesses love parties—especially cookie parties. These sugar cookies have a soft, airy texture that pairs perfectly with the sweet buttercream frosting, making them the ideal confection for any royal gathering. Make these cookies ahead of time, and let your partying princesses and princes do the frosting!

FOR THE DOUGH

1½ cups all-purpose flour

½ teaspoon kosher salt

¼ teaspoon baking powder

¼ teaspoon baking soda

¾ cups unsalted butter, softened

1 cup sugar

1½ teaspoons pure vanilla extract

2 large eggs

FOR THE FROSTING

½ cup unsalted butter, softened

1⅓ cups confectioners' sugar

1 teaspoon pure vanilla extract

Gel food coloring (color of your choice)

TO MAKE THE COOKIES: In a large mixing bowl, sift together the flour, salt, baking powder, and baking soda. Set aside.

In the bowl of a stand mixer fitted with the paddle attachment, beat the butter for 2 minutes, or until light and fluffy. Add the sugar and vanilla extract and beat for about 1 minute until fully incorporated. Add the eggs and beat for 1 minute more.

With the mixer running on its lowest setting, add the flour mixture a little at a time until just incorporated.

Transfer the dough to plastic wrap and form a log. Seal in the plastic wrap and chill in the refrigerator for 30 minutes.

Preheat the oven to 375°F. Line a baking sheet with parchment paper.

Remove the dough from the refrigerator and slice it into ¼-inch-thick pieces. Place on the parchment-lined baking sheet, leaving about 2½ inches between cookies. Bake for 10 to 12 minutes, or until golden brown at the edges. Let the cookies cool on the baking sheet for 3 minutes before transferring to a cooling rack to cool completely.

TO MAKE THE FROSTING: In the bowl of a stand mixer fitted with the paddle attachment, beat the butter for 2 minutes, or until light and fluffy. Add the confectioners' sugar and vanilla extract to the bowl and beat on low for 1 minute. Increase the speed to medium and beat for 2 to 4 minutes more, or until doubled in size.

TO DECORATE THE COOKIES: Add the desired food coloring to the frosting and mix well. Frost all the cookies with a thin layer of frosting and have fun decorating them. Sprinkles, edible glitter and other toppings can be used to customize the cookies, if desired.

Store in an airtight container at room temperature for up to 1 week.

SPRINKLE COOKIES

PRINCESS: JASMINE • YIELD: 24 COOKIES

As the daughter of a sultan, Jasmine spends her days hidden away in a palace while secretly longing to be free to see a whole new world. This caring, strong-willed Princess is always up for an adventure, and she gets her chance when Aladdin takes her for a breathtaking magic carpet ride. These cookies capture Jasmine's boldness and her signature colors. They are even rolled in sprinkles, giving them a unique and delightful texture that will surprise your guests and your taste buds!

2½ cups all-purpose flour
2 teaspoons baking powder
1 teaspoon salt
1 cup unsalted butter, softened
1¼ cups sugar
2 large eggs
1 teaspoon pure vanilla extract
¾ cup teal and gold sprinkles, mixed

Preheat the oven to 350°F. Line a baking sheet with parchment paper.

In a large mixing bowl, sift together the flour, baking powder, and salt.

In the bowl of a stand mixer fitted with the paddle attachment, cream together the butter and sugar. Mix on medium speed for 2 minutes, or until the mixture becomes light and fluffy. Add the eggs and vanilla extract and mix for about 1 minute more to combine. With the mixer running on its lowest speed, add the flour mixture to the butter mixture a little at a time until just combined.

Using a medium cookie scoop, scoop out cookie dough balls and roll them in sprinkles. Arrange on the baking sheet, leaving about 3 inches between cookies.

Bake for 10 to 12 minutes, or until golden brown at the edges.

Store in an airtight container at room temperature for up to 1 week.

EVANGELINE'S SPARKLING CINNAMON SUGAR COOKIES

PRINCESS: TIANA • YIELD: 24 COOKIES

Evangeline—the evening star in *The Princess and the Frog*—is beloved by Ray, the adorable firefly who pines for her, not realizing she is a star and not an insect like him. Evangeline was made from the spirit of a beautiful firefly. As an ode to her glittering beauty, these sparkling cookies are based on sugar cookies but have the heart of a snickerdoodle. They are buttery, cinnamony, and all-around delicious.

1½ cups all-purpose flour
1 teaspoon cinnamon
½ teaspoon baking soda
½ teaspoon baking powder
½ cup butter, softened
¾ cup sugar
1 large egg
½ teaspoon pure vanilla extract
Coarse gold sanding sugar

Preheat the oven to 375°F. Line a baking sheet with parchment paper.

In a large mixing bowl, sift together the flour, cinnamon, baking soda, and baking powder. Set aside.

In the bowl of a stand mixer fitted with the paddle attachment, cream together the butter and sugar. Beat for 3 minutes, or until light and fluffy. Add the egg and vanilla extract. Beat for 1 to 2 minutes, or until fully incorporated. With the mixer running on its lowest speed, add the flour mixture a little at time until just combined.

Use a small cookie scoop to scoop balls of dough onto the baking sheet, leaving 2 inches between cookies. Sprinkle with gold sugar.

Bake for 8 to 10 minutes, or until golden brown at the edges. Remove from the oven and let rest on a cooling rack until completely cool.

Store in an airtight container at room temperature for up to 1 week.

PART OF YOUR WORLD THUMBPRINT COOKIES

PRINCESS: ARIEL • YIELD: 24 COOKIES

Ariel is fascinated by all the things that humans use, from dinglehoppers to thingamabobs (she's got twenty, after all!). While she has always longed to be part of the world above the sea, this becomes especially important to her after she saves Prince Eric's life during a terrible storm. These enchanting cookies are made with a thumbprint of fruity jam to add a vibrant pop of color.

¾ cup unsalted butter, softened

½ cup sugar

2 large eggs

½ teaspoon pure vanilla extract

1 teaspoon salt

1¾ cups all-purpose flour, plus extra for dipping

¼ cup jelly, jam, or fruit preserves

Preheat the oven to 375°F. Line a baking sheet with parchment paper.

In the bowl of a stand mixer fitted with the paddle attachment, cream together the butter and sugar on medium speed for 2 minutes, or until light and fluffy. Add the eggs, vanilla extract, and salt and mix on medium for about 1 minute, or until combined. With the mixer running on its lowest speed, add the flour a little at a time until just incorporated.

Using a medium cookie scoop, scoop out balls of dough and place them on the baking sheet, leaving 2 inches between cookies.

Dip your thumb into flour, then press it into a ball. Repeat until all the cookies have thumbprints in the center. Fill the holes with your choice of jelly, jam, or preserves.

Bake for 10 to 12 minutes, until golden brown around the edges and on the bottom.

Let rest on a cooling rack until completely cool.

Store in an airtight container at room temperature for up to 1 week.

SABLE COOKIES

PRINCESS: BELLE • YIELD: 30 COOKIES

These traditional French cookies celebrate the land that Princess Belle hails from. The word *sable* means "sand," which is a fitting description for this dough: It is sandy in texture until it firms up in the refrigerator. With a light sweetness and smooth texture, these are delightful served with cocoa or other hot beverages.

2 cups all-purpose flour

1 cup confectioners' sugar

½ cup almond flour

½ teaspoon kosher salt

9 tablespoons cold, unsalted butter, cut into 1-tablespoon pieces

1 large egg, lightly beaten

Multicolored sanding sugar

In a large mixing bowl, sift together the flour, confectioners' sugar, almond flour, and salt. Add the cold butter to the flour mixture and use a pastry cutter or 2 knives to cut the butter into the flour until it resembles coarse crumbs. No large pieces of butter should be visible.

Make a well in the center of the flour mixture. Add the egg and use a fork to mix it in as best you can. It will not all come together at this point.

Turn the dough crumbs onto a clean cutting board or pastry board and knead together, using the heel of your hand to push the dough away from you and gather it back up. Continue until the dough forms a cohesive ball.

Transfer the dough to a piece of plastic wrap and form a 10-inch log that is even throughout. Roll completely to seal. Chill in the refrigerator for at least 3 hours.

Preheat the oven to 350°F. Line a baking sheet with parchment paper.

Remove the dough from the refrigerator and trim the ends. Slice it into ¼-inch slices, placing them on the baking sheet about 2 inches apart. Sprinkle with the sanding sugar. Bake for 15 minutes.

Transfer to a cooling rack and cool completely.

Store in an airtight container at room temperature for up to 1 week.

TRUE LOVE'S KISS COOKIES

PRINCESS: AURORA • YIELD: 24 COOKIES

When Aurora falls into a deep sleep after pricking her finger on a spinning wheel, the three good fairies, Flora, Fauna, and Merriweather, put the entire kingdom to sleep along with her. Only true love can wake the princess and break the curse. These buttery, sweet cookies are topped with a drop-shaped kiss—and they might just be true love for you, too.

1 cup unsalted butter, softened
1 cup confectioners' sugar
1 teaspoon pure vanilla extract
2 cups all-purpose flour
½ cup cornstarch
½ teaspoon kosher salt
24 drop-shaped chocolate candies, unwrapped
Pink sanding sugar

Preheat the oven to 375°F. Line a baking sheet with parchment paper.

In the bowl of a stand mixer fitted with the paddle attachment, add the butter, confectioners' sugar, and vanilla extract. Cream together until smooth, about 2 minutes.

In a separate bowl, sift together the flour, cornstarch, and salt. With the mixer running on its lowest speed, add the flour mixture to the butter mixture a little at a time, until just incorporated.

Use a medium cookie scoop to make 1-inch balls. Roll the balls in sanding sugar. Drop the cookies onto the prepared baking sheet, leaving about 2 inches between each cookie. Cook for 10 to 12 minutes, or until golden brown at the edges.

Immediately after removing the cookies from the oven, press a candy into the center of each cookie. Transfer the cookies to a cooling rack and cool completely.

Store in an airtight container in the refrigerator for up to 1 week.

ICED APPLE CIDER COOKIES

PRINCESS: SNOW WHITE • YIELD: 36 COOKIES

When the Evil Queen sets out to put Snow White into an eternal slumber, she comes prepared as an old woman bearing a beautiful, crimson-colored apple. Snow White gladly accepts it but soon falls prey to the deception. These cookies, frosted as red as Snow White's lips, pay homage to this infamous apple. They are filled with apple goodness and bathed in sweet icing.

FOR THE DOUGH

1 cup unsalted butter, softened

⅔ cup packed light brown sugar

½ cup sugar

2 cups chopped crispy apple chips

2 cups all-purpose flour

2 cups old-fashioned rolled oats (not instant)

2 teaspoon baking soda

1 teaspoon kosher salt

1 teaspoon cinnamon

½ cup apple cider

1 teaspoon pure vanilla extract

FOR THE GLAZE

1 cup confectioners' sugar

2 tablespoons milk

Red gel food coloring

FOR THE DECORATION

12 green gumdrops, cut into 36 leaves

TO MAKE THE COOKIES: Preheat the oven to 375°F. Line a baking sheet with parchment paper.

In the bowl of a stand mixer fitted with the paddle attachment, combine the butter, brown sugar, and sugar. Mix first on low and then on medium for a total of 3 minutes, or until the mixture is light and fluffy. Add the apple chips and mix briefly to combine.

In a medium mixing bowl, sift together the flour, oats, baking soda, salt, and cinnamon with a wire whisk. With the mixer running on its lowest speed, add the flour mixture little by little until fully incorporated, about 1 minute. Add the apple cider and vanilla extract and mix on low until the dough is smooth, about 1 to 2 minutes.

Use a medium cookie scoop, or 2 tablespoons, to drop the cookie dough in mounds on a prepared baking sheet.

Bake for 8 to 10 minutes until golden brown.

Transfer to a cooling rack and let cool completely.

TO MAKE THE GLAZE: In a small bowl, mix the sugar, milk, and food coloring. Brush the glaze on the cookies and add gum drop leaves. Let stand for 30 minutes.

For easy cleanup, set the cooling rack on a baking sheet lined with parchment paper before glazing.

Store in an airtight container at room temperature for up to 1 week.

MASSIVE CHUNKY PEANUT BUTTER COOKIES

PRINCESS: MERIDA • YIELD: 24 COOKIES

Self-assured, loyal, and a little bit rebellious, Merida comes from a kingdom of warriors where tables laden with food fuel everyone for their adventures across the Scottish countryside. These thick, chunky peanut butter cookies are made with chopped peanuts and peanut butter chips—perfect for keeping every peanut butter lover energized until the end of the party!

½ cup unsalted butter, softened
¾ cup creamy peanut butter
½ cup packed light brown sugar
¼ cup sugar
1 large egg
1 teaspoon pure vanilla extract
¼ teaspoon salt
1 teaspoon baking soda
1¾ cups all-purpose flour
1⅔ cups peanut butter chips
½ cup chopped honey-roasted peanuts

Preheat the oven to 350°F. Line a baking sheet with parchment paper.

In the bowl of a stand mixer fitted with the paddle attachment, cream together the butter, peanut butter, brown sugar, and sugar. Mix first on low and then medium for a total of 3 minutes, or until the mixture is light and fluffy. Add the egg and vanilla extract. Mix 1 minute more to combine.

In a large bowl, sift together the salt, baking soda, and all-purpose flour. With the mixer running on its lowest speed, add the flour mixture to the bowl a little at a time until just incorporated. Add the peanut butter chips and peanuts and mix briefly to combine.

Using a medium cookie scoop, scoop balls of dough onto the prepared baking sheet, leaving about 3 inches between cookies. Use a fork to create a crisscross pattern in the cookies.

Bake for 10 to 13 minutes, until the bottoms are golden brown and the centers are no longer moist.

Remove from the oven and cool for 3 minutes on the baking sheet. Transfer the cookies to a cooling rack and cool completely.

Store in an airtight container at room temperature for up to 1 week.

ALMOND COOKIES

PRINCESS: MULAN • YIELD: 36 COOKIES

When we first meet Mulan, she is trying her best to live up to the traditional expectations placed upon a young woman in her time. But her bold, adventurous spirit helps her break free from these restrictions as she takes her father's place in the Imperial Army. Although Mulan chooses to step away from tradition to protect her family, there are so many ways in which she honors it, too. These crunchy, flaky almond cookies are a traditional Chinese cookie filled with almond flavor and finished with an almond on top.

1⅓ cups almond flour

1 cup unsalted butter, softened

⅛ teaspoon kosher salt

2 large eggs

1 teaspoon almond extract

1¾ cups all-purpose flour

1 cup sugar, plus more for topping

½ teaspoon baking soda

36 almond slivers

In the bowl of a stand mixer fitted with the paddle attachment, beat the almond flour, butter, and salt at medium speed for 3 minutes, until the mixture resembles coarse crumbs.

Add 1 egg and the almond extract to the bowl and mix for 1 minute to combine. Add the flour, sugar, and baking soda. Mix on low speed until just incorporated.

Transfer the dough to a piece of plastic wrap and press it into a disk shape. Wrap thoroughly and chill in the refrigerator for at least 2 hours.

Preheat the oven to 325°F. Line a baking sheet with parchment paper.

In a small bowl, beat the remaining egg. Tear off small pieces of dough and roll them into balls about 1 inch in diameter. Place on the baking sheet and flatten with the palm of your hand. Place 1 almond sliver on each, then brush with the egg wash. Sprinkle with sugar.

Bake for 13 to 15 minutes, or until the edges of the cookies are golden brown. Transfer to a cooling rack to cool completely.

Store in an airtight container at room temperature for up to 1 week.

GINGER MOLASSES COOKIES

PRINCESS: RAPUNZEL • YIELD: 30 COOKIES

Even a Princess locked away in a tall tower has a busy schedule. Even with all her painting, knitting, reading, and, of course, brushing her hair, Rapunzel finds time to work on her baking. Then a charming thief flips her life upside down, bringing something unexpected to Rapunzel's days: fun! These spiced cookies have a bold flavor and soft texture. Their flavor is a bit unexpected as well, but in the best possible way!

- ¾ cup unsalted butter, softened
- 1 large egg
- 1 cup sugar, plus more for topping
- ¼ cup molasses
- 1 teaspoon pure vanilla extract
- 2¼ cups flour
- 1 teaspoon ground cinnamon
- 2 teaspoons ground ginger
- ½ teaspoon kosher salt
- 2 teaspoons baking soda

Preheat the oven to 350°F. Line a baking sheet with parchment paper.

In the bowl of a stand mixer fitted with the paddle attachment, beat together the butter, egg, and sugar for 2 minutes, or until light and fluffy. Add the molasses and vanilla and beat for 1 minute more until combined. The mixture should resemble mousse.

In a medium bowl, sift together the flour, cinnamon, ginger, salt, and baking soda.

With the mixer running on its lowest speed, add the flour mixture a little at a time until fully combined, about 1 minute.

Using a medium cookie scoop, scoop out balls of the dough and roll them in granulated sugar. Place them on the prepared baking sheet, leaving about 2 inches between each cookie.

Bake for 8 to 10 minutes. Let cool on the baking sheet for 3 minutes before transferring to a cooling rack to cool completely.

Store in an airtight container at room temperature for up to 1 week.

SNOWBALL COOKIES

PRINCESS: BELLE • YIELD: 18 COOKIES

One of the sweetest (and funniest) moments in *Beauty and the Beast* comes when Beast finally begins to let his guard down with Belle and enjoy himself a bit, letting loose during an impromptu snowball fight. These sweet, coconutty cookies are made to look like little snowballs, in all their fluffy goodness. Just remember, these aren't for throwing!

- 1¼ cups sweetened coconut flakes
- ¾ cup all-purpose flour
- ¼ cup almond flour
- 1¼ cups confectioners' sugar
- ⅛ teaspoon kosher salt
- 6 tablespoons unsalted butter, softened
- 1 teaspoon pure vanilla extract
- ½ teaspoon almond extract
- 4 teaspoons milk

Preheat the oven to 350°F. Line a baking sheet with parchment paper.

In the bowl of a food processor, add ½ cup coconut flakes, along with the flour, almond flour, confectioners' sugar, butter, vanilla extract, and almond extract. Pulse for 2 to 3 minutes, or until the dough comes together.

Break off small pieces of dough and roll each into a 1-inch ball. Place the balls on the baking sheet, leaving 1½ inches between them.

Bake for 13 to 15 minutes, or until golden brown at the edges. Remove from the oven and transfer the cookies to a cooling rack to cool completely.

In a shallow bowl, combine the remaining 1 cup of confectioners' sugar with the milk until the mixture forms a smooth, thick glaze.

Place the remaining ¾ cup coconut flakes in a second bowl.

Line a baking sheet with wax paper and set a cooling rack on top.

Working with 1 cookie at a time, dip into the glaze, fully coating the domed portion of the cookie. Let the excess glaze drip off before dipping the cookie in the coconut. Place on the cooling rack. Repeat for the remaining cookies. Let harden.

Store in an airtight container at room temperature for up to 1 week.

CHAPTER FOUR

BROWNIES AND BARS

BERRY GOOD GRANOLA BITES

PRINCESS: POCAHONTAS • YIELD: 8 SERVINGS (4 CUPS)

Free spirited and curious, Pocahontas always wants to know what's around the river bend. This adventurous spirit leads her to commune with nature and helps her learn to respect the lessons of Grandmother Willow. But a Princess on the go needs energy! Made with nuts, dried fruit, and grains, these bites are perfect for fueling adventures at home and in the outdoors.

- 2 egg whites
- 2 tablespoons light brown sugar
- 4 cups oat and honey granola
- ½ cup chopped pecans
- ½ cup dried cranberries
- ¼ cup chopped dried strawberries

Preheat the oven to 350°F. Line a 9-by-13-inch baking sheet with parchment paper.

In the bowl of a stand mixer fitted with the whisk attachment, beat the egg whites to soft peaks. Add the brown sugar and mix on medium for 1 minute until combined. Fold in the granola, pecans, dried cranberries, and dried strawberries.

Using a spatula, press the granola mixture onto the baking sheet until it's spread out evenly. Bake for 15 to 18 minutes, until golden brown.

Remove from the oven and transfer the parchment paper (with the granola mixture on top) to a cutting board. Gently cut shallow guidelines into bars (but don't separate them).

Cool completely and cut again, following the guides you cut. The bars will crumble when transferred to a container.

Store in an airtight container at room temperature for up to 1 week.

CHERRY COOKIE BARS

PRINCESS: MULAN • YIELD: 16 BARS

Channel Mulan's fighting spirit with these fruit-and-chocolate-inspired blondie bars. The sweet combination of cherry and dark chocolate makes these buttery cookie bars a favorite among partygoers. Best of all, they require only one bowl to make! Like clever Mulan, who works smarter, not harder while doing chores and protecting her family, these bars deliver a big payoff without a big amount of work.

- ½ cup unsalted butter, melted
- 1 cup packed light brown sugar
- 1 large egg, beaten
- 1½ teaspoons pure vanilla extract
- 1 teaspoon lemon juice
- ½ teaspoon baking soda
- ¼ teaspoon salt
- 1 cup all-purpose flour
- ½ cup dried cherries
- ½ cup dark chocolate chips

Preheat the oven to 350°F.

In a large mixing bowl, stir together the butter and sugar. Add the egg and vanilla extract and stir to combine. Add the lemon juice, baking powder, salt, and flour and stir again, until just combined. Fold in the dried cherries and dark chocolate chips.

Pour the batter into an 8-by-8-inch glass baking dish. Tap the pan on the counter or use a rubber spatula to gently even out the batter. Bake for 25 to 30 minutes, or until golden brown and dry on top.

Remove the bars from the oven and cool on a cooling rack for at least 10 minutes before slicing. For the most uniform cuts, cool completely before slicing into 16 squares.

Store in an airtight container at room temperature for up to 1 week.

DRAGON FRUIT CHEESECAKE BARS

PRINCESS: RAYA • YIELD: 12 BARS

Raya's father believed that their people could come together again if someone took the first step. Kumandra, their land, yielded plentiful fruits, such as spiked dragon fruit. And these sweet, creamy, and tart Dragon Fruit Cheesecake Bars could be the very thing to start rebuilding that trust. These are easy enough for any princess to make and are nearly no-bake!

2 cups honey graham crackers

½ cup unsalted butter, cut into pieces

½ cup sugar

Two 8-ounce package cream cheese, room temperature

1 teaspoon lemon zest

1 cup heavy cream

1 packet of gelatin, dissolved in ¼ cup cool water

1 cup frozen dragon fruit, defrosted

Preheat the oven to 400°F.

Combine the graham crackers and butter in the bowl of a food processor and process until coarse crumbs form. Press the crumbs into a 9-by-13-inch glass baking pan. Bake for 10 to 12 minutes, until lightly browned at the edges.

When the crust is out of the oven, combine the sugar with the cream cheese and lemon zest in the bowl of a stand mixer fitted with the whisk attachment. Beat on its lowest speed at first and then increase to medium speed and beat until smooth, about 2 minutes. Add the heavy cream and gelatin. Beat on the stand mixer's lowest speed until the cream begins to incorporate. Increase the speed to medium and beat until the mixture becomes thick and smooth, about 3 to 4 minutes. The cream cheese mixture should hold its shape when you lift the mixer head.

In a blender, purée the dragon fruit. Set aside.

Spoon the cream cheese mixture into the crust and spread it into an even layer. Drop the puréed dragon fruit by the spoonful all around the cheesecake topping. Swirl gently with a knife.

Chill, covered, for at least 2 hours before serving. Cut into 12 bars.

Store in an airtight container in the refrigerator for up to 3 days.

Poems and Fables
Fairy Tales

BOOKISH BROWNIE BARS

PRINCESS: BELLE • YIELD: 12 BARS

Brave, curious Belle is known to be intelligent and adventurous because of her love of books and reading. These rich, chewy, chocolaty brownie bars are decorated with bookish designs to celebrate her love of reading. Use different colors of frosting, and have fun creating a whole library of brownie books!

FOR THE DOUGH

½ cup unsalted butter

4½ ounces milk chocolate

1 cup sugar

½ cup packed light brown sugar

4 large eggs

1 teaspoon pure vanilla extract

1 cup all-purpose flour

¾ cup cocoa powder

½ teaspoon kosher salt

1 teaspoon baking powder

1 cup dark chocolate chips

FOR THE FROSTING

1 cup unsalted butter, softened

4 cups confectioners' sugar

1 teaspoon pure vanilla extract

¼ to ⅓ cup milk

Decorating gel or icing

TO MAKE THE BARS: Preheat the oven to 375°F. Spray a 9-by-13-inch baking pan with cooking spray.

In a small saucepan set over medium heat, melt the butter and chocolate together, whisking until combined. Remove from the heat. Let stand for 5 minutes.

In a large mixing bowl, whisk together the sugars and eggs. Drizzle in the chocolate, whisking constantly, until fully combined. Whisk in the vanilla extract.

In a separate bowl, sift together the flour, cocoa powder, salt, and baking powder. Add the flour mixture to the chocolate mixture and whisk well until combined. Fold in the dark chocolate chips.

Pour the batter into the prepared baking pan. Tap gently to even out the top.

Bake for 20 to 25 minutes, until baked through. Use a toothpick inserted in the center to determine whether the bars are ready: If the toothpick comes out clean, the brownies are done.

Let cool completely before making the frosting.

TO MAKE THE FROSTING: Add the butter to the bowl of a stand mixer and beat for 2 minutes, or until fluffy. Add the confectioners' sugar and vanilla extract and beat on low to combine. Add the milk little by little until achieving the desired consistency.

TO DECORATE THE BARS: Cut the brownies into 12 pieces. Frost each one. Use decorating gel or icing to draw book bindings on each one and write fun titles for all the books.

Store in an airtight container at room temperature for up to 1 week.

MAGIC BARS

PRINCESS: MERIDA • YIELD: 12 BARS

All around Merida, there is magic. When she's a child, the fabled will-o'-the-wisps lead her out of the forest and back to her parents. Later, she asks a witch for a cake that will change her fate so she doesn't have to be the good maiden who marries. This updated version of the classic magic bar won't change your fate, but it will make your taste buds very happy. These bars are a little less sweet than the classic version, but they're just as rich and delicious. With the addition of ginger snaps to the crust, there's an unexpected spice as well.

- 1 cup graham cracker crumbs
- ½ cup ginger snap crumbs
- ½ cup unsalted butter, melted
- One 14-ounce can sweetened condensed milk
- 2 cups dark chocolate chips
- 1½ cups sweetened coconut flakes
- 1 cup walnuts

Preheat the oven to 350°F. Spray a 9-by-13-inch glass baking dish with cooking spray.

In a medium mixing bowl, stir together the graham cracker crumbs, ginger snap crumbs, and melted butter. Pour the mixture into the prepared baking dish and press to form a single, even layer of crumbs. Pour the sweetened condensed milk over the top and spread it out. Sprinkle with chocolate chips, coconut, and walnuts. Pat gently to press the toppings down.

Bake for 25 to 27 minutes, or until golden brown. Cool completely and then cut into 12 triangles.

Store in an airtight container at room temperature for up to 1 week.

PECAN COOKIE BAR RAFTS

PRINCESS: MOANA • YIELD: 9 BARS

How far will Moana go to save her island and her people? As far as the ocean will let her! And she'll make some amazing friends along the way, even if they include a trickster demigod. These sweet, nutty Pecan Cockie Bar Rafts celebrate Moana's journey across the ocean with Maui to cure Te Fiti of its curse and bring balance back to her beloved island.

FOR THE BASE

½ cup cold unsalted butter, cut into pieces

¼ cup sugar

1¼ cups all-purpose flour

1 teaspoon pure vanilla extract

FOR THE TOPPING

1 cup packed light brown sugar

¼ cup unsalted butter, melted

1 large egg, lightly beaten

1 cup chopped pecans

TO MAKE THE BASE: Preheat the oven to 350°F.

Combine the cold butter, sugar, flour, and vanilla extract in the bowl of a food processor and process until coarse crumbs form. Pour the mixture into an ungreased 9-by-9-inch glass baking dish and press into a single layer.

Bake for 20 minutes. The edges should be slightly golden brown when you remove the base from the oven.

TO MAKE THE TOPPING: In a large bowl, stir together the brown sugar and melted butter. Add the egg and stir vigorously to combine. Mix in the pecans.

Pour the topping over the prebaked base of the bars. Bake for 30 to 35 minutes, until the topping is set in the center. Remove from the oven and let cool completely before cutting into 12 bars.

Store in an airtight container in the refrigerator for up to 5 days.

BAYOU BARS

PRINCESS: TIANA • YIELD: 16 BARS

When Tiana accidentally gets turned into a frog, she is shocked. And can we blame her? Her unexpected transformation leaves her trying just about everything she can think of to find her way back into her human form. Likewise, these sweet, chunky bars contain a little of everything, from chocolate chips to potato chips, creating a sweet and salty treat that's deliciously balanced.

½ cup unsalted butter, softened, plus more for greasing

½ cup packed light brown sugar

½ cup sugar

2 large eggs

2 teaspoons pure vanilla extract

2 cups all-purpose flour

2 teaspoons baking powder

1 teaspoon kosher salt

1 cup milk chocolate chips

1 cup yogurt-covered raisins

¾ cup crushed potato chips

¾ cup broken pretzels

Preheat the oven to 350°F. Grease a 9-by-13-inch glass baking dish with butter.

In the bowl of a stand mixer fitted with the paddle attachment, cream together the butter, brown sugar, and sugar for about 2 minutes, or until the mixture is light and fluffy. Add the eggs and vanilla extract. Beat for 1 minute to combine.

In a large mixing bowl, sift together the flour, baking powder, and salt. In a medium bowl, stir together the chocolate chips, yogurt-covered raisins, potato chips, and pretzels.

With the mixer running on its lowest speed, add the flour mixture little by little until just incorporated. Add 2 cups of the chocolate chip mixture and mix briefly to incorporate.

Transfer the dough to the prepared baking dish. Press it into a single, even layer that stretches from end to end. Sprinkle with the remaining chocolate chip mixture.

Bake for 22 to 25 minutes, or until golden brown. Cool completely before cutting into 16 bars.

Store in an airtight container at room temperature for up to 1 week.

UNDER THE SEA BLONDIE BARS

PRINCESS: ARIEL • YIELD: 16 BARS

The colors in Ariel's kingdom are simply magical, from the soft tan sand of the ocean floor to the pastels of coral, seaweed, and sea creatures. Why not celebrate this with your own Under the Sea Princess Party, featuring a viewing of *The Little Mermaid* and complete with mermaid tails, Shell Cookie Sandwiches (page 117), and Starfish Cookies (page 28)? And, of course, you'll want to serve these sweet, buttery bars—with their light frosting, they are decorated to represent the many colors of the sea where Ariel swims.

FOR THE DOUGH

½ cup unsalted butter, melted, plus more for greasing

½ cup packed light brown sugar

1 large egg, beaten

1½ teaspoons pure vanilla extract

½ teaspoon baking powder

¼ teaspoon salt

1 cup all-purpose flour

½ cup white chocolate chips

FOR THE FROSTING

½ cup unsalted butter, softened

2 cups confectioners' sugar

1 teaspoon pure vanilla extract

Turquoise gel food coloring

2 tablespoons milk

6 tablespoons mermaid sprinkles

TO MAKE THE BARS: Preheat the oven to 350°F. Grease an 8-by-8-inch glass baking dish with butter.

In a large mixing bowl, stir together the butter and brown sugar. Add the egg and vanilla extract and stir to combine. Add the baking powder, salt, and flour and stir again, until just combined. Fold in the white chocolate chips.

Pour the batter into the prepared baking dish. Tap the pan on the counter or use a rubber spatula to gently even out the batter. Bake for 25 to 30 minutes, or until golden brown and dry on top.

Remove the blondies from the oven and cool completely.

TO MAKE THE FROSTING: Combine the butter, confectioners' sugar, vanilla extract, food coloring, and milk in a bowl. Beat with a handheld mixer until creamy. This can also be done in the bowl of a stand mixer fitted with the whisk attachment. Spread on the blondies and top with sprinkles. Let stand for 20 minutes before slicing into 16 brownie bites.

Store in an airtight container at room temperature for up to 1 week.

PISTACHIO COOKIE BARS

PRINCESS: JASMINE • YIELD: 16 BARS

These cookie bars are dedicated to Princess Jasmine, who longs to be free and to see the world. Rich and nutty, these pistachio cookie bars are easy to make in a single bowl and taste a bit less sweet than many other cookies. They are the perfect complement on your party table to the sweeter cookies, such as Nameplate Cookies (page 31) and Walnut Baklava (page 124).

½ cup unsalted butter, melted

½ cup packed dark brown sugar

½ cup sugar

1 large egg, beaten

1 teaspoon pure vanilla extract

½ teaspoon baking powder

¼ teaspoon salt

1 cup all-purpose flour

½ cup chopped pistachios, plus 2 tablespoons for sprinkling

Preheat the oven to 350°F.

In a large mixing bowl, use a handheld mixer to cream together the butter, brown sugar, and sugar. Add the egg and vanilla extract and mix to combine. Add the baking powder, salt, and flour, and stir again, until just combined. Fold in ½ cup of chopped pistachios.

Pour the batter into an 8-by-8-inch glass baking dish. Tap the pan on the counter or use a rubber spatula to gently even out the batter. Sprinkle with the remaining 2 tablespoons of pistachios. Bake for 25 to 30 minutes, or until golden brown and dry on top.

Remove the blondies from the oven and cool on a cooling rack for at least 10 minutes before slicing. For the most uniform cuts, cool completely before slicing into 16 squares.

Store in an airtight container at room temperature for up to 1 week.

CHAPTER FIVE

SPECIALTY COOKIES

MERINGUE PRINCESS WANDS

YIELD: 12 WANDS

Need a little bibbidi-bobbidi-boo in your life? These fun and fantastical wands are easy to make, although they do take a little longer than many of the other recipes. Get creative with edible glitter dust, or add a little gel food coloring to make these wands in different colors. You can also change up the flavor by substituting almond or strawberry extract for the vanilla extract. Then pull on your best princess gown to complete the look!

2 egg whites

1 teaspoon pure vanilla extract

⅛ teaspoon kosher salt

⅛ teaspoon cream of tartar

½ cup sugar

Edible glitter dust in different colors

Preheat the oven to 200°F. Line a baking sheet with parchment paper.

In the bowl of a stand mixer fitted with the whisk attachment, beat the egg whites, vanilla extract, salt, and cream of tartar at medium speed until soft peaks form. Continue mixing, adding the sugar very slowly, until stiff peaks form.

Add the meringue to a piping bag fitted with a star tip. Pipe 12 dots onto the prepared baking sheet and place one lollipop stick on each one. Pipe a star or a heart on top of each stick.

Bake for 2 hours. Turn off the oven and let the meringues stand inside the oven for 45 minutes.

Remove from the oven and let the meringues cool before taking them off the baking sheet. Transfer to a cooling rack. When fully cooled, use a clean, food-safe paintbrush to dust the wands with edible glitter dust in the colors of your choice.

Store in an airtight container at room temperature for up to 1 week.

TUK TUK BROWN SUGAR OATMEAL COOKIES

PRINCESS: RAYA • YIELD: 24 COOKIES

Raya's best friend, Tuk Tuk, is part pill bug, part pug, and all sweetness, just like these rich, sweet oatmeal cookies. Super fun to serve for a *Raya and the Last Dragon* viewing party, these cookies are made to look like the loyal friend and traveling buddy of this brave Princess.

1¼ cups all-purpose flour
1 teaspoon baking powder
½ teaspoon kosher salt
1 teaspoon cinnamon
1 cup unsalted butter, softened
1 cup packed light brown sugar
½ cup sugar
2 large eggs
1 teaspoon pure vanilla extract
2 cups old-fashioned rolled oats (not instant)
1 cup raisins (optional)
Candy eyes

Preheat the oven to 375°F. Line a baking sheet with parchment paper.

In a large bowl, sift together the flour, baking powder, salt, and cinnamon. Set aside.

In the bowl of a stand mixer fitted with the paddle attachment, cream together the butter, brown sugar, and sugar, first on low speed and then on medium, for a total of 2 minutes. The mixture should be light and fluffy when ready. Add the eggs and vanilla extract to the bowl. Mix for 1 minute on medium, or until fully incorporated.

With the mixer running on its lowest speed, add the flour mixture little by little until just incorporated. Add the oats and raisins, if using, and mix briefly to combine.

Use a medium cookie scoop to drop balls of the dough onto the prepared baking sheet, leaving about 3 inches between cookies. Bake for 12 to 14 minutes, or until golden brown. Remove from the oven and press 2 eyes into each cookie while the cookies are warm.

Let cool for 3 minutes on the baking sheet, then transfer to a cooling rack to cool completely.

Store in an airtight container at room temperature for up to 1 week.

WEDDING COOKIES

PRINCESS: CINDERELLA • YIELD: 24 COOKIES

After all the heartache and struggle, Cinderella finally gets her happy ending with the Prince and escapes her stepmother and stepsisters. Dressed in all white, like these sweet, crumbly, tender cookies, Cinderella is the picture of grace and poise. Try these when you are looking to add a bit of elegance to your next get-together.

½ cup unsalted butter, softened
1 cup plus 2 tablespoons confectioners' sugar
1 teaspoon pure vanilla extract
1½ cups finely chopped pecans
1 cup all-purpose flour
1 large egg

Preheat the oven to 325°F. Line a baking sheet with parchment paper.

In the bowl of a stand mixer fitted with the paddle attachment, cream together the butter and 2 tablespoons of the confectioners' sugar, about 2 minutes. Add the vanilla extract, pecans, and flour to the stand mixer and mix on the lowest speed until well combined, about 1 minute. Add the egg and mix thoroughly until the dough comes together, about 1 minute.

Using a medium cookie scoop, scoop the dough onto the baking sheet, leaving about 1 inch between cookies.

Bake for 20 to 22 minutes, until lightly golden around the edges.

Remove from the oven and immediately transfer the cookies 1 at a time to a bowl with the remaining 1 cup of confectioners' sugar. (Note: The cookies are fragile at this point, so touch them as gingerly as possible.) Gently roll to coat with the sugar and transfer to a cooling rack set over a baking sheet to catch any excess sugar. Continue until all the cookies are coated. Sprinkle any remaining sugar over the cookies. Let cool completely before enjoying.

Store in an airtight container at room temperature for up to 1 week.

SHELL COOKIE SANDWICHES

PRINCESS: ARIEL • YIELD: 16 SANDWICHES

Two sweet, soft sugar cookies conceal a swirl of rich chocolate buttercream and a secret: an edible pearl. There's so much to be found in Ariel's under-the-sea world, including surprises like this. Every bite is a chocolaty, buttery treat that your Princess Party guests will adore.

FOR THE DOUGH

¾ cup unsalted butter, softened

1¼ cups sugar

1 teaspoon pure vanilla extract

2 large eggs

1½ cups unbleached all-purpose flour

½ teaspoon kosher salt

¼ teaspoon baking powder

FOR THE FROSTING

¼ cup unsalted butter, softened

1 cup confectioners' sugar

¼ cup unsweetened cocoa powder

½ teaspoon pure vanilla extract

2 tablespoons milk

SPECIAL INGREDIENTS

Edible pearls

Madeleine pan (optional)

Preheat to 375°F. Line a baking sheet with parchment paper.

TO MAKE THE COOKIES: In the bowl of a stand mixer fitted with the paddle attachment, cream together the butter, sugar, and vanilla extract on medium speed for 2 minutes, or until the mixture is light and fluffy. Add the eggs and beat for about 1 minute more, until well combined.

In a medium bowl, sift together the flour, salt, and baking power. With the stand mixer running on its slowest speed, add the flour mixture a little at a time until just incorporated.

Use a small cookie scoop to place scoops of dough onto the baking sheet, leaving about 3 inches between cookies. Or, if you are feeling a bit fancy, add dough to a Madeleine pan for seashell-shaped cookies (pictured in photo).

Bake for 10 to 14 minutes, until the edges are just beginning to brown. Cool completely.

TO MAKE THE FROSTING: In the bowl of a stand mixer fitted with the whisk attachment, cream the butter until light and fluffy. Add the confectioners' sugar, cocoa powder, and vanilla extract. Beat on low until crumbly. Add the milk, a little at a time, with the mixer running on low. When all the milk has been added, increase the speed to medium and beat until fluffy.

Transfer the frosting to a pastry bag fitted with a star tip. Pipe small mounds of frosting onto half the cookies. Top each with another cookie, angling it so the cookie sandwich looks like an open shell. Press an edible pearl into the frosting and serve.

Store in an airtight container at room temperature for up to 5 days.

CORNBREAD COOKIES

PRINCESS: POCAHONTAS • YIELD: 24 COOKIES

Cornbread lovers will adore the soft, crumbly, lightly sweetened flavor of these delicate cookies, which pay homage to one of the most important crops to Pocahontas and her people: corn. This is an excellent recipe to make when you gather with your little bakers for your next Princess Cookie Party.

¾ cup unsalted butter, softened

¼ cup sugar

½ cup packed dark brown sugar

1 large egg

1 teaspoon pure vanilla extract

¾ cup cornmeal

1 teaspoon baking powder

½ teaspoon salt

¾ cup all-purpose flour

Preheat the oven to 350°F. Line a baking sheet with parchment paper.

In a large bowl or the bowl of a stand mixer, add the butter, sugar, and brown sugar. Cream together using a handheld mixer or a stand mixer fitted with the paddle attachment, about 2 minutes. Add the egg and vanilla extract and mix well for about 1 minute.

In a medium bowl, sift together the cornmeal, baking powder, salt, and flour.

With the mixer running on low, add the dry ingredients to the wet ingredients a little at a time until completely combined.

Use a medium cookie scoop (or 2 spoons) to drop 1-tablespoon rounds onto the baking sheet, leaving about 1 inch between cookies.

Bake for 10 to 12 minutes, or until lightly browned.

Transfer to a cooling rack to cool completely.

Store in an airtight container at room temperature for up to 5 days.

STRAWBERRY LYCHEE COOKIES

PRINCESS: RAYA • YIELD: 24 COOKIES

There are so many delightful fruits in Raya's world, including lychees, which Tuk Tuk is seen carrying in a basket. These sweet, fruity cookies combine the delicate flavor of lychee and the floral goodness of strawberries for an unexpected and bold cookie.

1¼ cups unbleached all-purpose flour
1 teaspoon baking soda
½ teaspoon kosher salt
½ cup unsalted butter, softened
½ cup packed light brown sugar
½ cup sugar
1 large egg
1 teaspoon lychee flavor extract
1 cup chopped dried strawberries
Red and pink sanding sugar

Preheat the oven to 350°F. Line a baking sheet with parchment paper.

In a large mixing bowl, add the flour, baking soda, and salt. Use a whisk to sift together. Set aside.

In the bowl of a stand mixer fitted with the paddle attachment, combine the butter, brown sugar, and sugar. Beat on medium until smooth, about 2 minutes. With the mixer running on its lowest speed, add the egg and lychee flavor extract. Slowly add the flour mixture, 1 spoonful at a time, until fully incorporated. Add the strawberries and mix until just combined.

Use a medium cookie scoop to drop the dough into even rounds on the prepared baking sheet, about 2 inches apart. Sprinkle with sanding sugar.

Bake for 10 to 13 minutes, or until the cookies are lightly browned. Let cool for 5 minutes before transferring to a cooling rack to cool completely.

Store in an airtight container at room temperature for up to 1 week.

HEART OF TE FITI COOKIES

PRINCESS: MOANA • YIELD: 36 COOKIES

Moana is on a mission to return the Heart of Te Fiti to save her island and her people. These rolled cookies are made to look like that prized gem she carries with her during her journey. Beware, though: This dough is a bit sticky, so it's essential to chill it thoroughly, even between baking cookie batches.

1 cup unsalted butter, softened
1 cup sugar
1 large egg
½ teaspoon kosher salt
2 teaspoons pure vanilla extract
2½ cups all-purpose flour
¼ cup milk
Green and blue gel food coloring

In the bowl of a stand mixer fitted with the paddle attachment, cream together the butter and sugar until light and fluffy, about 2 minutes. Add the egg, salt, and vanilla extract. Beat on medium to combine, about 1 minute. With the mixer running on its lowest speed, add the flour little by little until fully combined. Add the milk and beat for 1 to 2 minutes until fully combined.

Divide the dough in half, adding green food coloring to one half and blue food coloring to the other. Wrap each ball of dough in plastic wrap and pat into even rectangles. Chill in the refrigerator for 1 to 2 hours.

Remove the dough from the refrigerator, unwrap, and stack both pieces of dough on a floured piece of wax paper. Using a rolling pin, roll into a 10-by-14-inch rectangle. Roll on the long side into a log. Wrap the log in plastic wrap, rolling out slightly, if needed, to achieve uniform thickness.

Chill in the refrigerator for 1 to 2 hours.

Preheat the oven to 350°F. Line a baking sheet with parchment paper.

Remove the dough from the refrigerator and trim the ends. Slice into ¼-inch rounds. Place about 2 inches apart on the prepared baking sheet. Bake for 14 to 16 minutes, or until golden brown at the edges. Wrap any extra dough and chill in the refrierator between batches.

Let the cookies cool on the baking sheet for 3 minutes before transferring them to a cooling rack to cool completely.

Store in an airtight container at room temperature for up to 1 week.

WALNUT BAKLAVA

PRINCESS: JASMINE • YIELD: 16 PIECES

When Jasmine disguises herself to sneak out of the palace gates, she finds a whole world of flavors, textures, personalities, people, and problems she didn't know existed. It reinforces her desire to be a part of the greater world—not just her palace life. This traditional sweet pastry is made up of layers of buttered phyllo dough and a nut mixture to form a bold dessert worth sharing!

1 cup unsalted butter,
melted, plus more for greasing

1 pound walnuts

⅓ cup granulated sugar

½ tablespoon cinnamon

½ teaspoon freshly ground black pepper

One 16-ounce package phyllo dough

1 cup water

1 cup sugar

½ cup honey

2 teaspoon pure vanilla extract

Preheat the oven to 350°F. Butter a 9-by-13-inch glass baking dish.

In the bowl of a food processor, pulse the walnuts in batches until finely chopped. Transfer to a mixing bowl and stir together with the cinnamon and pepper.

Lay 2 pieces of phyllo dough in the buttered dish and brush with butter. (Note: If using large sheets of phyllo, fold them in half to achieve 2 layers.) Repeat, 2 slices at a time, until 8 pieces of phyllo have been stacked. Sprinkle with ½ cup of the nut mixture. Top with 2 pieces of phyllo and butter, followed by another 2 pieces and butter, and then another 2 pieces and butter. Top with ½ cup of the nut mixture. Repeat until all the nut mixture has been used. The top layer of the baklava should be 6 to 8 slices thick and buttered on top.

Using a sharp knife, cut on the diagonal, leaving 1 inch between cuts. Repeat in the opposite direction to form a diamond pattern.

Bake for 45 to 55 minutes, until golden brown.

When the baklava is just about done, combine the water, sugar, honey, and vanilla extract in a small saucepan and heat over medium heat, stirring constantly. Simmer for 5 minutes or until the mixture becomes translucent.

Remove the baklava from the oven and pour the syrup mixture over the top, taking care to spread it evenly.

Let stand, uncovered, for at least 4 hours before recutting and serving.

Store in an airtigh container in the refrigerator for up to 5 days.

SCOTTISH SHORTBREAD

PRINCESS: MERIDA • YIELD: 16 PIECES

Fiery and brave, Merida longs to buck tradition in her kingdom and be a warrior like her father. She is a horse-riding, bow-shooting fierce young woman. But some traditions are too good to pass on, like traditional Scottish shortbread. These crumbly cookies are subtle but fierce and also not too sweet—kind of like Merida herself.

2 cups all-purpose flour
1 cup unsalted butter, softened
¼ cup sugar
¼ cup packed light brown sugar
¼ teaspoon kosher salt

Preheat the oven to 350°F. Spray an 8-by-8-inch glass baking dish with cooking spray.

In the bowl of a food processor, combine the flour, butter, sugar, brown sugar, and salt and pulse until the mixture looks like soft breadcrumbs that hold together when pinched.

Pour the mixture into the prepared dish and press into an even layer. Prick all over. Use a dough scraper to precut the dough into 1-by-2-inch rectangles.

Bake for 30 to 35 minutes, or until golden brown. Remove from the oven and cool completely before cutting.

Store in an airtight container at room temperature for up to 1 week.

BLUEBERRY BEIGNETS

PRINCESS: TIANA • YIELD: 24 BEIGNETS

Tiana dreams of opening her own restaurant one day, a vision she and her father created years ago. In New Orleans, where she lives, the traditional cuisine includes beignets, powdered donut-like pastries that are fried to perfection. This creative version adds sweet wild blueberries to the mix, making these confections as distinctive as they are tasty!

3 cups all-purpose flour
1 teaspoon kosher salt
3 tablespoons sugar
1 cup whole milk, warmed
2¼ teaspoons active dry yeast (¼-ounce packet)
1 large egg
3 tablespoons butter, melted
2 quarts vegetable oil
3 cups confectioners' sugar
½ cup frozen blueberries

In the bowl of a stand mixer fitted with the paddle attachment, sift together the flour, the salt, and 2 tablespoons of sugar.

In a medium mixing bowl, add the warm milk and sprinkle with the remaining 1 tablespoon of sugar and the yeast. Let stand for 5 minutes, or until foamy.

Add the egg to the yeast mixture and beat together until well combined. Add to the flour mixture. Run the mixer on medium-low for about 1 minute, or until a wet, shaggy dough forms.

Change the stand mixer attachment to the dough hook. Add the melted better and run the mixer on medium-low for about 1 minute, or until the butter is fully incorporated. Increase the mixer speed to medium-high and knead for about 6 minutes, or until the dough is cohesive and tacky.

Transfer the dough to a greased bowl. Cover with a dish towel and let rise for about 2 hours, or until doubled in size.

Add the oil to a 4-quart pot and heat over medium heat. Place a cooling rack on top of a baking sheet near the stove, along with a bowl of the confectioners' sugar and tongs.

Turn the dough onto a floured surface and spread it out. Top with ¼ cup of the blueberries and fold to combine, adding the other ¼ cup after the first fold. Use a rolling pin to roll the dough out into a 10-by-14-inch rectangle. Cut into 24 pieces. Cover with a dish towel while the oil heats.

The oil is ready when it reaches 340°F. Drop in several beignets at a time, taking care not to crowd the pan. Fry for 3 to 4 minutes per side, flipping once, until golden brown all over. Remove to the cooling rack and let cool for 2 minutes before tossing in the confectioners' sugar.

Repeat for the remaining dough. Be sure to check the oil temperature periodically because it may need time to be reheated after a few batches.

These are best eaten fresh.

Store (minus the confectioners' sugar) in an airtight container for up to 3 days. Heat and sprinkle with confectioners' sugar just before serving.

ROYAL BALL TUILES

PRINCESS: CINDERELLA • YIELD: 12 COOKIES

What does one serve at a Royal Ball? Why, the most delicate confections possible, of course! These thin rolled cookies are dipped in chocolate for a delightful treat that's perfect for Cinderella's first Royal Ball.

- ¾ cup all-purpose flour
- 1 cup confectioners' sugar
- ⅛ teaspoon kosher salt
- ½ cup unsalted butter, melted and slightly cooled
- 4 large egg whites, room temperature
- 1 teaspoon pure vanilla extract
- 4 ounces milk chocolate

In a medium mixing bowl, sift together the flour, confectioners' sugar, and salt. Add the butter and whisk to combine. Add the egg whites and vanilla extract and whisk again to combine. When the mixture is smooth, cover with plastic wrap and chill in the refrierator for 1 hour.

Preheat the oven to 400°F. Line a baking sheet with parchment paper.

Drop 2 teaspoons of batter onto the baking sheet and use a spreader to smooth it into a very thin 5-inch circle. Repeat to make a second circle, spacing them about 5 inches apart. (Note: Bake only 2 cookies at a time). The cookies are ready when the edges begin to color.

Remove from the oven and transfer 1 cookie to a cooling rack. Wrap it around the handle of a wooden spoon to form a cylinder, then carefully remove the spoon handle and repeat with the second cookie.

Repeat for the remaining batter. Let the cookies cool completely on a cooling rack.

Break the chocolate into pieces and place them into a microwave-safe bowl. Microwave for 30-second intervals on high, stirring after each one, until smooth. Do not overheat.

Dip the cookie ends into the chocolate and place them on a baking sheet lined with wax paper to harden.

Store in an airtight container at room temperature for up to 3 days.

MAGIC LAMP CHOCOLATE PISTACHIO BISCOTTI

PRINCESS: JASMINE • YIELD: 10 BISCOTTI

Jasmine is one smart cookie. When Jafar tries to get the Genie to make Jasmine love him, something the Genie cannot do, Jasmine flirts with Jafar so Aladdin can retrieve the magic lamp. Like the magic lamp, these Chocolate Pistachio Biscotti are also pretty flashy, with their layer of chocolate plus more chocolate inside—not to mention pistachios. These take a bit longer to make than most cookies, but just like Jasmine's deception, they are worth the wait. Biscotti are crisp cookies best served with a hot beverage for dipping.

2 cups all-purpose flour

⅔ cup sugar

1 teaspoon baking soda

½ teaspoon salt

1 cup mini semisweet chocolate chips

½ cup chopped pistachios

1 teaspoon pure vanilla extract

2 large eggs

1 large egg white

4 ounces milk chocolate

Preheat the oven to 350°F. Line a baking sheet with parchment paper.

In a large mixing bowl, stir together the flour, sugar, baking soda, salt, chocolate chips, and pistachios. Set aside.

In a smaller bowl, use a handheld mixer to beat together the vanilla extract, eggs, and egg white until combined.

Pour the egg mixture into the dry ingredients and stir until mostly combined. The dough will be crumbly and will not come together fully.

Turn the dough onto a floured work surface and knead with floured hands until it forms a smooth ball.

Place the dough on the prepared baking sheet and pat it into a 1-inch-thick piece, pushing the ends in until it appears rectangular in shape.

Bake for 30 to 35 minutes, until golden brown at the edges.

Remove from the oven and transfer to a cutting board. Cut the biscotti into ½-inch slices. (It helps to score the log with a serrated knife and then use an extra-sharp knife to cut straight down.) Place the slices on the baking sheet.

Bake for 10 minutes. Flip all the slices and bake for 10 minutes more. Cool on the baking sheet for 5 minutes, then transfer to a cooling rack to cool completely. The biscotti harden as they cool.

When cooled, break the chocolate into pieces in a microwave-safe bowl. Microwave for 30 seconds, stir, and microwave for 30 seconds more, or until just melted.

Dip each piece of biscotti in the chocolate and place, chocolate side down, on a baking sheet lined with wax paper to cool completely.

Store in an airtight container at room temperature for up to 1 week.

LUMIÈRE'S GRAY STUFF COOKIES

PRINCESS: BELLE • YIELD: 12 COOKIES

Go ahead, try the gray stuff! When Lumière brings Belle a plate of confections, you can't miss the swirl of gray stuff included with the other hors d'oeuvres. This creamy gray stuff tastes like a chocolate sandwich cookie and is a great complement to salty crackers.

4 ounces cream cheese, softened

4 tablespoons unsalted butter, softened

1 teaspoon pure vanilla extract

1¼ cups confectioners' sugar

1 teaspoon milk (optional)

3 chocolate sandwich cookies

24 round butter crackers

In a stand mixer fitted with the paddle attachment, combine the cream cheese, butter, and vanilla extract. Mix on low and then on medium until smooth, about 2 minutes.

Add the confectioners' sugar to the bowl and mix on low for 1 minute. Increase the speed to medium and mix for 3 to 4 minutes more, or until firm and fluffy. If the mixture is too thick, add milk a little at a time to reach the desired consistency.

Crush the chocolate sandwich cookies, then mix them into the frosting.

Chill for 15 minutes.

Transfer to a piping bag and pipe onto the butter crackers in swirls. Enjoy immediately.

Store in an airtight container in the refrigerator for up to 5 days. Bring to room temperature and pipe onto the crackers just before serving.

KISS A FROG COOKIES

PRINCESS: TIANA • YIELD: 24 COOKIES

Would you kiss a frog if it meant finding your prince? Tiana does, and, although the path to her prince was a bit more complicated than she expected (and filled with many close calls with the swamp gators), in the end, she and Prince Naveen live happily ever after. Celebrate Tiana's journey with these green crinkle cookies, which have a soft, comforting texture and are packed with vanilla flavors.

1½ cups all-purpose flour
½ teaspoon baking soda
½ teaspoon baking powder
½ cup unsalted butter, softened
1 cup sugar
1 large egg
1 teaspoon pure vanilla extract
½ teaspoon green gel food coloring
¼ cup confectioners' sugar

Preheat the oven to 375°F. Line a baking sheet with parchment paper.

In a medium mixing bowl, sift together the flour, baking soda, and baking powder. Set aside.

In the bowl of a stand mixer fitted with the paddle attachment, cream together the butter and ¾ cup of the sugar until light and fluffy, about 2 minutes at medium speed. Add the egg, vanilla extract, and food coloring and mix for about 1 minute more to incorporate fully.

With the mixer running on its lowest setting, add the flour little by little until fully incorporated.

Using a small cookie scoop, drop balls of dough into the remaining ¼ cup of sugar, turning to coat them. Transfer to a bowl with the confectioners' sugar, again turning to coat. Repeat until all the cookies are coated in the 2 sugars.

Place on the prepared baking sheet, leaving 1½ inches between cookies.

Bake for 8 to 10 minutes, or until golden brown at the edges.

Store in an airtight container at room temperature for up to 1 week.

QUEEN ELINOR'S TASSIES

PRINCESS: MERIDA • YIELD: 22 TASSIES

Like her mother, Merida is fiercely dedicated to her family and her kingdom. They are also both stubborn and strong and have soft hearts, not unlike these adorable tassies. Crusty on the outside, they look like mini pecan pies, but inside they are gooey and delightful. The rich cream cheese–based crust is perfect for the nutty filling.

FOR THE DOUGH

½ cup unsalted butter, softened

4 ounces cream cheese, softened

1 cup all-purpose flour

1 teaspoon sugar

⅛ teaspoon kosher salt

FOR THE FILLING

1 tablespoon unsalted butter, melted

¼ cup light brown sugar

¼ cup maple syrup

1 large egg, lightly beaten

½ teaspoon pure vanilla extract

⅛ teaspoon kosher salt

½ cup chopped pecans

TO MAKE THE TART CRUSTS: Preheat the oven to 350°F. Spray the cavities of a mini muffin pan with cooking spray.

In the bowl of a stand mixer fitted with the paddle attachment, combine the butter and cream cheese. Beat on medium until combined, about 2 minutes. Add the flour, sugar, and salt and beat until a soft dough forms, about 1 to 2 minutes.

Working with about 1 tablespoon of dough at a time, roll the dough into balls and place into the mini muffin cavities. Press the dough into the cavities, ensuring it reaches up the sides to the top.

TO MAKE THE FILLING: In a large mixing bowl, use a handheld mixer to cream the butter, brown sugar, and maple syrup until well combined. Add the egg, vanilla extract, and salt and stir vigorously to combine. Fold in the pecans.

Divide the mixture evenly among the tart crusts, taking care not to overfill them; it will be difficult to remove the tassies if the filling spills over.

Bake for 20 to 25 minutes, or until the tops are golden brown. Cool in the pan for 5 minutes and then remove to a cooling rack.

Store in an airtight container at room temperature for up to 1 week.

ACKNOWLEDGMENTS

Writing a cookbook is an incredible experience that begins with imagination and ends with words on a page that hopefully convey the desired experience to an audience. In between are many days and nights of recipe testing, many batches of cookies, and many opinions.

I could not have undertaken this project without the help of my community. Seriously, this was a group effort. Thank you to my children, Will and Paige, for tasting so many of the recipes and creating the cookie distribution network that insured we weren't drowning in baked goods for the early book-writing process. Thank you also to my many friends, neighbors, and colleagues who lent taste buds and opinions to this book, especially Julia Bayly, Melissa Gerety, James Gerety, Izzy Harrow, Reagan Monroe, Patrick O'Brien, Gibran Graham, and the Smiley family; the staff of Barliman's in Bangor, Maine; the staff of The Briar Patch in Bangor, Maine; my Husson University colleagues; my brother, Zach, and his wife, Ariel; and so many others in Maine, Connecticut, and beyond. Seriously, this was a massive group effort. Thank you to my whole family for their unwavering support.

Special thanks to my editor, Eileen Mullan, who was a steadfast partner in this massive undertaking and who encouraged me to tap into creativity throughout the book. Thanks for being my partner in princesses!

Finally, thank you to the one who didn't blink when I said "I think I am going to agree to this cookbook, even though it's a little outside my normal work and that other book is also due." Your steady and steadfast belief in me across time and space is the buoy I didn't know I needed. You once said to me that you never forgot how much I loved to write and that you were so happy I turned that love into a career—as I said I would. Thank you for noticing, thank you for watching, thank you for bringing out the best version of me.

ABOUT THE AUTHOR

For more than two decades, Sarah Walker Caron has been writing about food for websites, magazines, newspapers, news sites, and books. Now the author of twelve books, including *The Pizza Planet Cookbook*, *Disney Princess Tea Parties*, and *Harry Potter and Fantastic Beasts: Official Wizarding World Cookbook*, she specializes in quick and easy cooking from scratch and aims to encourage home cooks to get into the kitchen more.

In 2005, she founded Sarah's Cucina Bella (www.sarahscucinabella.com) to begin her food writing journey. No one is more surprised than she is that it's still going strong more than twenty years later, but she adores her readers and loves sharing her recipes.

In addition to food writing, Sarah teaches journalism at the University of Maine and Husson University. She's also a Pushcart Prize–nominated essayist, former newspaper editor, and longtime freelance writer. Her work has appeared in dozens of outlets including The Girlfriend, SheKnows, Betty Crocker, Tablespoon, and *Fine Cooking*.

INDEX

INSIGHT EDITIONS
PO Box 3088
San Rafael, CA 94912
www.insighteditions.com

Find us on Facebook: www.facebook.com/InsightEditions
Follow us on Instagram: @insighteditions

ISBN: 979-8-3374-0374-8

Publisher: Raoul Goff
SVP, Group Publisher: Jeff McLaughlin
VP, Manufacturing: Alix Nicholaeff
Associate Publisher: Thom O'Hearn
Art Director: Stuart Smith
Senior Designer: Brooke McCullum
Senior Editor: Eileen Mullan
Editorial Assistant: Melissa Santoyo
Managing Editor: Shannon Ballesteros
Production Editor: Ivy Long
Production Manager: Deena Hashem
Strategic Production Planner: Lina s Palma-Temena

Photography by Waterbury Publications, Inc.

ROOTS of PEACE REPLANTED PAPER

Insight Editions, in association with Roots of Peace, will plant two trees for each tree used in the manufacturing of this book. Roots of Peace is an internationally renowned humanitarian organization dedicated to eradicating land mines worldwide and converting war-torn lands into productive farms and wildlife habitats. Roots of Peace will plant two million fruit and nut trees in Afghanistan and provide farmers there with the skills and support necessary for sustainable land use.

Manufactured in China by Insight Editions

10 9 8 7 6 5 4 3 2 1